HIS

PASSIONATE

PURSUIT

Victoria Boyson

HIS

PASSIONATE

PURSUIT

Published by XP Publishing
P. O. Box 1017
Maricopa, Arizona 85139
XPPublishing.com

ISBN: 978-1-621660-10-1

Printed in the United States of America. For Worldwide Distribution.

Contents

For Ellen

"The rain and snow come down from the heavens
and stay on the ground to water the earth.

They cause the grain to grow, producing seed
for the farmer and bread for the hungry.

It is the same with my word.
I send it out, and it always produces fruit.

It will accomplish all I want it to,
and it will prosper everywhere I send it."

Isaiah 55:10-11 NLT

Introduction

GOD IS PURSUING you – running to embrace you as He did in the parable of the Prodigal Son. He doesn't care what you've done, He just wants you, His dearly loved child, back in His arms. He wants you with Him, where you are safe and where He can love you the way He designed you to be loved.

As He embraces you, He releases His glorious presence into your life, letting it flow to you from His heavenly throne. You become a beacon of light, a fountain of life and a gateway for the power of heaven to touch the earth.

As I was writing *His Passionate Pursuit*, I continually encountered God in a way that was earnest, and I felt Him pouring out His heart to His family. It was His letter declaring the love He has for you. This book is God describing His dreams for an intimate relationship with you.

This is not just a book but a portal of heaven unleashing His presence into your life that will empower you with an impartation from heaven.

I know God will captivate your heart. You will encounter your heavenly Father in a way that will change your life as He invests Himself in you.

Get ready for a life-changing encounter with God!

1

Passionate Pursuit

IN A VISION, I was with God in the Spirit as we flew over the surface of the earth. He held me as we traveled at tremendous speed, causing everything on the earth's surface to appear as if it were one massive blur.

As we traveled together, I felt the passion in the Lord's heart. He was utterly determined to find someone who was yearning for Him – one whose heart was reaching out to find Him.

After some time of flying at this speed, we slowed down and focused in on one lone woman who was on her knees crying out to God in desperate prayer. I watched the Lord as He stood in front of the precious woman and gazed down at her, but she didn't seem to know He was there. As she prayed, the Lord breathed in deeply to take in the aroma of her prayers. He closed His eyes and raised His head. His chest heaved as He breathed. His eyes brimmed with tears as He became enveloped in the sweet fragrance of her prayers.

As He drew in her prayers, radiant light began to burst forth from inside Him. The light seemed to be electrified, with waves of power surging through it. It burst out from Him and encircled both He and the woman in what seemed like a cocoon of magnificent light.

As I watched, I marveled at this remarkable moment. The Lord then spoke to me and said, "It was her desperation for Me that drew Me to her."

"They Want Me!"

Years ago, I took part in a church service where the passion of our worship was very high; you could feel the heightening of our longing for our Lord. Many people were crying out to God in desperate anticipation of Him.

"Come, Lord Jesus! You are welcome here!" they cried. As our worship increased, our longing for Him intensified.

I felt in my spirit that the Lord was truly moved by our desire for Him. He spoke to my heart like an emotional bridegroom, "Look, Victoria, they want Me!" Our longing for Him gripped His heart.

I burst into tears with my head in my hands, not because I was sad but because He was so happy. I was delighted for Him - delighted to see His heart made so full by the sincere and ardent worship of those He loved so much. It was as though we were at last beginning to desire Him even as He longs for us.   WOW

Our hearts were captivated by Him because we were suddenly made aware of our great need of Him and of the emptiness we had inside us without Him. We felt His desperation and His love for us. We knew that He wanted to be with us, and our response to Him was "Come, Lord, come!"

God is passionately seeking those who are awakened to His heart and yearning for His presence. He watches for the moment when you turn to pursue Him, because He is pursuing you. As you turn to Him, His heart skips a beat as He watches you in breathless anticipation, hoping you come to Him. He's passionate for you to realize how much you desperately need Him.

Who Is It You Are Looking For?

Mary Magdalene was one who truly loved Jesus. To her, He was not just the Savior of the world, He was her Friend. To this woman who had lived a difficult and rejected existence, He represented hope. He represented the only faithfulness and love she had ever known. Jesus was the only one who had treated her with care and respect. He made her feel she really mattered to Him. Instead of seeking what He could take from her, Jesus set her free from all bondage she had endured in her life, and then He poured His life into her. So she loved Him.

When Jesus was crucified and buried, it was Mary who woke before the sun to run to His tomb (see John 20:1). And with her heart crushed, it was she who stayed by His tomb crying when His body could not be found.

When the two angels stationed at the tomb asked her why she was crying, she replied, "They have taken my Lord away and I don't know where they have put him" (John 20:13).

The sight of the angels before her didn't stun her. Undeniably, her only thought was for her Lord. Can you imagine her pain? Her only Friend, the only One who truly loved her and gave her hope, was singled out and killed – she'd lost Him. She was desperately unhappy and when Jesus appeared to her, she did not recognize Him. Overcome by emotion, she broke down and wept uncontrollably.

Jesus was overwhelmed by her heartfelt display, and He spoke to her.

"Woman, why are you crying? Who is it you are looking for?" Thinking he was the gardener, she said, "Sir, if you have carried him away, tell me where you have put him, and I will get him."

.—John 20:14-15

She had seen Him, the One she loved, brutally tortured and killed. She had watched in a state of shock and despair as the unthinkable happened. In her bewilderment, she endured the countless questions in her mind as He suffered. *Is this what He meant when He said something would happen to Him? Was this what He was talking about?*

Through the agony of her mind, she wondered if it were all just a bad dream. He had helped so many. How could they possibly kill Him? She could not force her mind to think or let herself reason; all she knew was that the One she loved was dying. Then suddenly, He was gone.

Mary carried all her heartache with her to the tomb that Sunday morning. She rushed there the very moment it was permitted. When she arrived, she found more heartache still ... His body was missing!

She wanted to hold Him and care for Him just as He had cared for her. Now even this she could not do – she could not even find His body. This was too much for her to take; she could no longer bear it. Under the weight of her grief, she broke down and wept.

In her broken desperation, she cried to the man she thought was the gardener. "Sir, where is He?"

Drawn by Her Passion

Jesus had yet to present Himself to His Father, but He felt Mary's cries of despair, so He went first to comfort her. To Mary, a simple soul who'd known very little but heartache in life, He would show Himself first. He had not seen His heavenly Father nor His own mother, yet His heart responded to the despondent cries of a woman whose heart was desperately longing for Him.

She did not recognize Him...so He asked her, "Who is it you are looking for?" (John 20:15).

He knew who she was looking for; He did not need to ask her. Her passionate grief for Him was what had drawn Him to her. Jesus simply wanted to hear her say it. He wanted to hear *who* it was she was searching for. He wanted to hear her say the words, "Sir, if you have carried him away, tell me where you have put him, and I will get him" (v.15).

How her words must have revived Him; He went from the arms of His accusers to the passionate pursuit of His friend. He could no longer hold back His compassion for her and He revealed Himself to her.

"Mary," He said.

"Rabboni!" she cried.

She had unsuccessfully searched for His lifeless body, but now she found Him whole. Suddenly, Mary was transformed from desperation and agony to exuberant joy! She had found the One whom her soul longed for.

In her passion, she lunged at Him, embracing Him. But Jesus grabbed her and said, "Do not hold on to me, for I have not yet ascended to the Father" (John 20:17). But she couldn't help it. The dark night she had lived through had passed and a bright morning had come in its place.

"I Will Be Found by You"

The Lord is looking for those who are ardently seeking Him, whose hearts are longing for Him – those who love Him. He is desperately looking for those like Mary who are desperate for Him and who want to be with Him. When He finds one who is passionately seeking Him, someone who wants Him, He explodes with excitement. It is what He's dreamt of since the Garden of Eden, for He longs to walk with us as He walked with Adam and Eve.

"'You will seek me and find me when you seek me with all your heart. *I will be found by you*,' declares the Lord" (Jeremiah 29:13-14). That is His promise to you.

Beloved, the One your heart longs for will come to you! Turn your eyes toward Him. He is desperate for you. You will see how truly amazing His love is for you and how much He desires to pour His life into you.

2

Historic Romance

AS WE GROW from childhood into adulthood, we often determine our own self-worth by how we are treated by those around us. For instance, if we are continually treated as though we do not matter, regardless of what the truth is, we will develop a mindset that we are of little value. It's difficult to unlearn the negative things taught to us in early life, but that is exactly what we must do. Until we are able to shake our minds free from the opinions of man, we will not be able to receive God's truth about ourselves. His truth is the only truth that's real and the only one that matters.

You are very important to God and He wants you to know just how much you mean to Him. When you understand how much He loves you, you are set free from the bondage of your past.

So, open your heart and focus on this truth, for it is truly how He feels about you:

On the precious day God planned for your birth, heaven waited with Him in anticipation, and suddenly you were born. Enraptured with you, He cried and danced – He joyfully shouted and threw His arms in the air.

In elation over you, He roared with joy to all of heaven, "Look at that! Did you see that?" And all of heaven joined Him in His joy over you.

From that moment until this, His thoughts have been with you – waiting – planning – praying – hoping – loving. He wanted you and has pursued you. You are His fervent desire. His heart is overflowing with expectation for all the adventures He has planned to share with you.

As you grew, He could see more of His dream unfolding – He planned you from the beginning of time and now you are here. When you took your first steps, He cheered you on. When you ran, He ran beside you. And when He sees you begin to walk in your destiny, He rallies the cheering crowds of heaven to shout for joy over you. He's seriously captivated by you, that is why He made you – to celebrate you. → that sounds

Heaven celebrates you!   radical to me

You are His joy and He wants you to discover who He *really* is, not just what you've been told about Him.

When you begin to see your Father as He actually is, you will discover who you really are.

This is your historic romance! Heaven's history will tell your story and you will see how much joy you've brought to heaven as you've embraced the One who loves you more deeply than you could ever realize. It's His story of the love of His life ... *you*!

Understanding God's Love

He loves you as only the dearest Father can. His love is pure and reliable – untainted by human circumstances. He created you to enjoy you. He sought you out to love you. And because He loves you, He wants you to know Him personally – He loves you too much to let you live your life experiencing Him only from a distance.

When you experience His love and truly enjoy a relationship with Him, you enter a realm of faith that has no room for myth or legend – this faith is a reality. You learn to trust Him – to lean on Him – to count on Him. Suddenly, you can trust Him to love you the way He created you to be loved.

God's love for you is powerful, and receiving it enables you to receive His blessings as well. Experiencing His love for you causes you to live an expectant life of watching and waiting to see how He reveals His joy in you simply because you are His.

The Piano Recital

When my oldest child, Cassandra, was only four years old, she started piano lessons. Every year her teacher had a Christmas recital for her students to show how much they had improved.

Cassandra was her youngest student, and her talent was not yet developed. The first song she played was "Mary Had a Little Lamb." Everyone knew that song, of course, so they recognized immediately when she played a wrong note, which she did ... frequently. She'd shake her head as if to say, "No, I didn't mean to play that note." But, she continued playing to the end.

As her mother, I took joy in every note, good or bad. Her timing was off, but to me every note she played was magical and beautiful. To me, her performance was perfection and I was extremely proud.

Cassandra's performance was thrilling to me not because she was perfect but because she was my daughter. Because she was mine, I saw her as the star of the program. And I will never forget the moment: the way her hair hung in a mass of beautiful curls – the way her legs dangled, swinging back and forth off the front of the bench – how she struggled to get off the bench when she was finished.

Because she was my daughter – because she belonged to me – I beamed with pride as she finished her contribution to the program that evening. As she sat next to the older children, just like a big girl, I could hardly hold back tears.

Why was I so thrilled at Cassandra's performance? Why did she touch me so? Because she was *my* daughter – *she belonged to me*. I enjoyed Cassandra because she was mine!

With as much enjoyment and pride I had as I watched Cassandra, your heavenly Father watches you with even *greater delight*, because you belong to Him. You are *His* child. He is so proud of you and He enjoys even the little things you do. *really?*

How terrible it would have been if I had scolded Cassandra for her missed notes and bad timing; but to me even her off-notes were beautiful. Likewise, no matter how you feel you have missed it, your heavenly Father *is* proud of you. Whenever He wants to brighten up His day … He looks at you.

In the company of angels, He speaks proudly of you. He beams with pride and declares to all of heaven, "That's My child! That's My child! Doesn't he … doesn't she … look just like Me?"

His Passion

He is motivated in every action by His love for you. When you are wounded, it grieves Him deeply. When you forgive, He beams with pride. When you miss it, He's your cheerleader saying, "Come on, you can do it…keep trying…don't give up!" Even when you are caught in sin and face the consequences of it, it hurts Him even more than it hurts you.

Even when you are at your very worst, He wants you to run into His arms and receive His abundant grace and favor for your life. That is what grace means: it means you can run to Him even when you've done wrong.

He will *never* throw in the towel or give up hope of you becoming the person He has always dreamed you would be. Why? Because you are His, and He not only sees your potential, but He feels it in every fiber of His being. When He sits and thinks, He dreams about the day you begin to walk in your destiny; it is what gives Him joy.

It is God's desire that you see Him as your heavenly Father. It was His plan, His design, and His desire for you to see Him as a truly loving Father who cares about everything you do.

Satan wants you to recoil from knowing God as Father. He wants you to believe God is standing over you with judgment, waiting to condemn you for every mistake. But, God is the One who stands in your corner calling out to you, His beloved child. He says to you,

> *My son, My daughter, I love you! You can overcome ... I have given you the keys to the kingdom. Defeat your enemy and stand. Stand in My love – stand in My grace – stand in My favor. You will succeed!*

Transformed by Christ's Love

The Samaritan woman Jesus found at the well in John 4:1-29 was thirsty when she met Him. She was thirsty, but what was she really thirsty for? She'd never found anything in her life that had brought her fulfillment. Her happiness was always short-lived – going from man to man. She didn't realize it, but her thirst was for her Messiah – for the freedom only He could give her, and now that she'd met Him, she would never thirst again.

When she realized she'd found the Messiah, she was overwhelmed and freed from the shame she'd lived with her whole life. Experiencing His intense, life-transforming love, she *had* to share it:

> Then leaving her water jar, the woman went back to the town and said to the people, "Come, see a man who told me everything I ever did. Could this be the Messiah?" They came out of the town and made their way toward him.   —John 4:28-30

The eyes of the villagers were opened when they saw this forlorn woman who, being rejected by many, was transformed by Christ's love. She was no longer afraid of the rejection of the people; she did not need their acceptance anymore, for she had experienced His. Jesus had accepted her, so their approval was irrelevant. Rejection could not touch her; she didn't care what others thought anymore. She'd found her value *in Christ.*

He had seen *everything she'd ever done,* but did not judge her ... He transformed her.

"Come see a man," she told the people. Jesus uncovered the shameful things of her past, and then erased them all. She no longer had to hide from her past – it was forgiven. A life full of death had now received new life. No more forlorn, now she was loved. Once rejected by them, *now she led the townspeople to find what she had found:* Life!

They saw the change in her. They heard her words, and something deep inside them was awakened by a desperate hope. Could they know Him like she knew Him, they wondered? Would He accept them as they were, an abandoned, rejected society of Samaritans? Could He be the One their hearts had longed for? Could He fill their emptiness? The answer is an overwhelming "Yes!"

You have a Father who adores you! He wants to embrace you and spend every moment of every day with you. It is with Him, in His presence, that you are made complete. He is the greatest love you will ever know.

Jesus is pleading with you,

Stop seeking after the world, which can never be enough for you, and look to Me. I am the only one who can truly love you, the world cannot.

You were not made for this world. God made you for Himself and He's planted in your DNA the need for a connection with Him. He knows that apart from Him your life is filled with pain and darkness. He loves you enough to pursue you passionately – to draw you to Himself.

He was pursuing you when He sent His Son to die on your behalf. Driven by love, He sent Jesus. "For *God loved* the world so much that he gave his one and only Son, so that everyone who believes in him will not perish but have eternal life" (John 3:16 NLT). He pursued you before you even knew you were lost. Nothing the world has can compare to this. So why care if this world loves you or hates you? You have all that you will ever need in *His* arms.

So often, when distracted by life, I don't realize what it is I'm missing. I feel "off," but I can't understand what's wrong. Then He comes to me and stills my heart. He turns my face to meet His gaze, and my heart is content to receive His love for me. In His presence I can never get enough of Him; I don't want to leave Him. I don't want to sleep or wake. I only want to stay with Him.

Once He has my attention, I can finally release the pain of my heart and surrender myself completely to Him. And the more I understand His love for me, the more I am able to give Him everything, receiving His perfect peace in return.

Turn Your Gaze

Can He fill the emptiness in your heart? Yes ... He longs to!

Let Him turn your gaze away from this chaotic world and give you lasting peace.

Surrender your heart to Him; He will love you. Perhaps many have rejected you, and you feel unattractive and unloved inside. He wants you to see yourself through the mirror of His grace.

"You are truly beautiful," He cries.

Listen to the words of that wonderful song, "Turn your eyes upon Jesus, look full in His wonderful face. And the things of earth will grow strangely dim, in the light of His glory and grace."[1] The Lover of your soul is asking you to turn toward Him. "Look on me," He says, "you are mine and I love you. I am your source. Don't seek acceptance from any other."

The decision is yours. He wants you; He's made your way clear by giving His Son for you. He wants to

---

[1] "Turn Your Eyes upon Jesus," Helen H. Lemmel, 1922

know if you want Him, too. Meet Him in this passionate pursuit. Let His gaze bring healing and wholeness to the deepest regions of your heart. He is the One your soul longs for. He is yours and you are His. He is all you need. You were made for Him...

Arise, come, my darling; my beautiful one, come with me.   —Song of Songs 2:13

3

Relentless Love

Once you were far away from God, but now you
have been brought near to him through the blood
of Christ.   —Ephesians 2:13 NLT

THE ENEMY'S LIES about you can keep you from
experiencing a close relationship with God. You may
even think his lies are your own opinions, but they
could be the tools the enemy is using to keep you from
living fully in God's love. Even one lie can keep you in
bondage in some area of your life and hinder you from
walking fully in ALL that God has for you.

God saw you when you were without hope. You may
not have even realized you were lost or that there was a
way out of the loneliness and pain you felt – it seemed
normal to you to feel that way, but when God looked at

you, He saw royalty. He chose you for His own – to be a part of Himself – to be protected and loved.

Indeed, His relentless love *pursues* you continuously. And He will never stop His passionate pursuit of you until He has *all* of your heart. He's determined to rescue you from the entanglements and snares that keep you from embracing Him more freely.

He wants to transform you *from* being rejected and uncared for – *to* being the dearest child of His heart. He wants to show the world the realities of what He is in you, manifesting His glory through you. Truly, He sees you as valuable and worthy. He sees your possibilities. And He has set a table before you in the presence of your enemies (see Psalm 23:5).

> Even before he made the world, God loved [you] and chose [you] in Christ to be holy and without fault in his eyes.
>   —Ephesians 1:4 NLT, emphasis mine

He is relentless in His pursuit of you. He's committed to your full transformation through His grace and mercy until you are made blameless, reflecting His image. That is how much He loves you.

Always Remembered

The realization that God is truly pursuing you, even when you've run from Him, can literally change your life. It's when you've failed God, and we all have failed Him, that you begin to truly feel and appreciate His unconditional love. When you think of His extravagant pursuit of you it can be very humbling. It strips away any pretense or self-righteousness, beautifully placing your hope firmly in the work of the Cross.

In Luke 7:36-50, Jesus was invited to the home of a Pharisee. When a woman who'd lived a sinful life heard He was there, she bought an alabaster jar of very expensive perfume and went to see Jesus. When she found Him, she wept, wetting His feet with her tears. She wiped them with her hair, kissed His feet and sweetly poured perfume on them.

It was the tradition at the time to offer your guests water to wash their feet and anoint them with oil, but this was not offered to Jesus when He entered the Pharisee's home. Yet, this dear woman who had lived a very sinful life, poured out her most costly fragrance on Him, weeping at His feet and drying her tears with her hair.

As usual, the Pharisees objected to this woman even touching Jesus, so He told them a parable of two debtors who owed money to a moneylender; one owed $500 and the other owed $50. When the moneylender forgave them both their debts, it was the one who owed more that appreciated the forgiveness more. Then Jesus declared to all the men present that this precious woman, as sinful and insignificant as she seemed, would be remembered for her love, not them. "I tell you, her sins – and they are many – have been forgiven, so she has shown me much love. But a person who is forgiven little shows only a little love."

She'd given her all from the depths of her heart, not knowing if she would be accepted and not caring. She became God's special treasure because of her act of passionate adoration for Jesus. And Christ said, "What this woman has done will always be remembered." For eternity Christ will brag on her, and this precious woman, who the Pharisees saw as unfit to touch Him, showed them how to truly love.

Peter's Failure – God's Trophy

Like the woman with the fragrance, Peter loved Jesus profoundly and had sworn to protect Him with his life (John 13:37). Peter wanted to be a trustworthy friend and servant to Him. He truly meant it when he said, "Even if all fall away on account of you, I never will" (Matthew 26:33 NIV). Peter wanted to stand by Him more than anything, but unfortunately that is not what he did.

In fact, when Jesus needed him the most, Peter denied even knowing Him (John 18:15-27). What inexpressible anguish he must have felt and how painfully he regretted his actions. He loved Jesus so much, yet he did what he did not want to do and failed to do what he wanted so much to do.

Having failed Him, what would he then decide to do? Would he walk away from Jesus, covered in shame and living without Him? Or would he humble himself, admit his failure and ask for forgiveness? He had to make a choice. He could emotionally beat himself up with self-loathing, or accept the mercy of Christ.

Peter proved he truly loved Jesus by humbling himself and receiving the forgiveness He offered. And on the day of Pentecost it was Peter who led thousands of people to the same arms of mercy in which he'd found forgiveness and restoration (Acts 2:14-40). Peter stood firmly in the forgiveness and unconditional love of God because he had experienced it. And through it, Peter received great authority to proclaim the truth of Jesus to the multitudes. Indeed, Peter became God's trophy – an emblem of His grace – to show him off to the world.

Relentless Pursuit

To those around you, you may seem insignificant. But your heavenly Father sees much more in you. He can see deep into the regions of your heart, and what He sees takes His breath away. He saw you and decided that He must have you for His own; He is driven by His love for you. He sees you as His workmanship ... His masterpiece, His dear friend.

God is not looking for a holier-than-thou – got-it-all-
together person to redeem. No, His idea of a masterpiece
is to take a life that has been wounded or locked in guilt
by shame, yet completely relinquished into His hands.
And even from the onset of His restoration work in your
life, He has empowered you to do His mighty works.

He sees you as a carrier of His presence. He's made
you a container for His Spirit, filled with His presence
because you love to spend time with Him. Indeed, you
carry His presence and through you He shows the world
"the incomparable riches [power] of His grace" (Ephesians 2:7).

Truly, if others can see what God's power has done .
in you, they will be drawn to Him because of you. If
they can see the power of His grace in you, they can be
rescued from the darkness that surrounds them.

Pursued by Your Grace

God pursues you to impart His grace to you, but the
subject of grace is difficult for many to receive. Grace is
truly one of the most powerful forces in existence, but it
is often disregarded as minor, because it is freely given.

For it is by grace you have been saved, through
faith – and this is not from yourselves, it is the
gift of God.   —Ephesians 2:8 NIV

Why does grace cause stumbling at times? It's difficult to understand God's unfailing love. We feel that God should love us for some reason, not just because He chooses to. We measure His love by our own human love, and it just doesn't compute.

In Matthew 20:1-16, the Lord explained grace to His disciples through the parable of the workers in the vineyard. In this message, the owner of a vineyard had hired several men early in the day to work for him for a denarius ($20) each. He went out at various times during the day to hire more men who needed work. He even went out at the "eleventh hour" and hired more men to work for him, though there was just a short time left in the day for them to work.

Why did the landowner continuously pursue more workers? Did he really have that much work to do? No, he pursued them to bless them. And God is pursuing you now, not because He wants something from you but because He wants to bless your life.

Sometimes it's difficult to accept His love because we're not sure we deserve it. Well, we don't. But it would hurt Him terribly if we denied His love. To receive His grace is humbling, and some don't like being humbled. That's why the Word says, "It is easier for a camel to go through the eye of a needle than for someone who is rich [proud] to enter the kingdom of God" (Matthew 19:24, emphasis mine).

Yet, if we refuse His grace, we are alienated from Christ. "You who are trying to be justified by the law [or by self-justification] have been alienated from Christ; you have fallen away from grace" (Galatians 5:4, emphasis mine).

However, the more you know Him and develop a friendship with Him, the easier it will be to receive His grace. As you get to know Him, He becomes much more to you than your Redeemer, He becomes your Friend. And as His friend, you learn to accept His unfailing love without having to understand why He loves you the way He does.

One thing I do understand about God is that His love is truly unfailing. Because it does not fail, He cannot stop pursuing what He loves. He absolutely refuses to fail. So, He continues His relentless pursuit until you are restored to Him, body and soul. Until you are filled with His Spirit and completely overflowing with His love, He will not stop pursuing you. He is relentless!

The Chapel – *A Vision*

Years ago I had gone through several traumatic events, and I felt overwhelmed by the reality of the painful incidents that had occurred. It left me feeling emotionally numb, unable to even cry. I could barely muster a prayer, yet my heart was crying out to God for His help.

I felt the Lord comforting me and holding me. He was desperately pursuing me, reaching out to soothe and encourage. But, because I had been treated so badly by those who should have loved me, I found it difficult to believe I was worthy of the love I needed, even God's love.

I cried out to the Lord to show me His love ... He did! He gave me a vision:

He held me in His arms as I encountered His Spirit. Suddenly, I saw heaven; I saw it as clear as if I were physically standing in it. There were rolling green hills in every direction, with large beautiful trees dotting the landscape. As I stood on top of one of the endless hills, I saw a small simple chapel nestled in the valley below. I knew in my spirit that I just had to get to it, and suddenly I was there.

The chapel looked very old but was obviously well cared for. Through the windows of the chapel I could see a light glowing from inside; I was compelled to go in. I opened the door at the back of the chapel and stood there for a while, absorbing the warmth from the light inside.

The chapel was empty except for one man who was praying at the altar. An amber glow filled the area where he knelt. I had a strong desire to see who it was and instantly I was at the front of the chapel looking at the man who was kneeling there.

He was crying as he prayed, and he seemed desperate to touch the heart of the Father. He prayed with such earnestness that I was curious to find out what he was praying for. He did not appear to know that I was there, so I moved closer to him. As I saw his face streaming with tears in deep intercession, I heard him say, "Father, please help Victoria." I gasped. He was praying for me.

It was then that I recognized who this man was ... it was Jesus.

The man praying in earnest was my Jesus, and I was the subject of His prayers. He was crying and interceding for me. I felt His overwhelming love for me — and His desperation. He was desperate for me to be delivered from the depression that had gripped my life.

I stepped back from the Lord and tried to process all that I was seeing. I was completely stunned. Who was I that Jesus would intercede for me and with such earnestness? Was I really that special to Him? Did He really love me that much? *Why would He take all this time by Himself, just to pray for me?* But, "He is able to *save completely* those who come to God through him, because he always lives to intercede for them" (Hebrews 7:25, emphasis added). It was difficult for me to fathom His intense love for me.

I sat for a while at the back of the church, watching Him pray. Suddenly, He stood up and turned and looked at me. He saw I was there and ran to me. Falling at my knees, He reached to embrace me, but I was still in such shock that I could not return His embrace. He looked at me with such intense love that it shook me from the numbness that gripped me, and I felt fully the love I was experiencing.

My eyes were opened and now I could see and feel His love for me. I still didn't understand His love, but *I knew then that I was very precious to Him.* And His love for me didn't stop with salvation, but He continues to save me every day.

You Are Very Special

If you were important enough for God to send His own Son to die for you, then you can believe that you are precious enough for Jesus to intercede for you. He gave Himself for you once in death, and He gives His life in intercession for you now.

If God is for us, who can be against us? He who did not spare his own Son, but gave him up for us all – how will he not also, along with him, graciously give us all things? Who will bring any charge against those whom God has chosen? It is God who justifies. Who then is the one who condemns? No one. Christ Jesus who died – more than that, who was raised to life – is at the right hand of God and is also interceding for us.

—Romans 8:31-34

He is *for* you, NOT against you! He is the One trying to convince you that it is possible for you to do great things for His glory. And, "If God is for us, who can be against us?" (Romans 8:31). The answer is: NO ONE CAN!

Who shall separate us from the love of Christ? Shall trouble or hardship or persecution or famine or nakedness or danger or sword?

—Romans 8:35

For I am convinced that neither death nor life, neither angels nor demons, neither the present nor the future, nor any powers, neither height nor depth, nor anything else in all creation, will be able to separate us from the love of God that is in Christ Jesus our Lord.   —Romans 8:38-39

He died for us that we might live for Him. Yet now He prays for us that we would possess all of Him! He saves us completely, not just at our redemption; He desires our complete transformation. He knows this is the only chance we have of truly living, to become one with Him in every aspect of our lives – giving our all to Him and watching Him transform us into all He's destined for us to be.

That moment when I was permitted to see Him interceding for me changed my life. And I hope that reading about this experience will also have an impact on your life. You are very special to God and He wants you to know it. It is not conceited to think that you are special. You are not just another face in the crowd to Him. You are what He died for.

You are His priceless treasure!

4

"Follow Hard After Me"

For me, to live is Christ and to die is gain.
—Philippians 1:21

THE LONGER I LIVE the more I realize that living a life hand-in-hand with the Beloved is a life profoundly lived. Loving Him makes you feel alive and fills your life with intense purpose. But the more vibrant your relationship is with Him, the more sinister the darkness of this present world seems in contrast. Christ's love in you sparks intensely felt love in the spirit realm, and those sparks light the night of the days we live in.

Your intimacy with Him is meant to make others jealous; it's not just for your benefit, but that the world might see the richness of His grace and grow in Him. It's romance on another level. It is a truly compelling relationship and has the power to change the world.

As you revel in the happiness you find in Him, you may not even realize you are being transformed. As you enjoy your Beloved, your soul is fashioned and shaped by His grace into a special piece of His heart – making you one with Him. You are made a part of His intensely passionate heart – united with Him in all He loves.

A Higher Purpose

Truly, your love for Him creates an instant eternal bond with those who love Him as you do. For in loving Him, you are no longer content to live for yourself but are compelled to surrender your life for a much higher purpose. You are now living for the entire kingdom of God, on earth as well as in heaven, and grasping this truth can create a fearless resolve.

Your love for Him forces you to overcome your fears, fashioning you into a brand new creation (2 Corinthians 5:17). You see the world through the eyes of your love for Him and it so overwhelms you that you are now driven by that precious love; fear is inconsequential.

Through love, you see clearly the value of what is eternal and temporal. Your life here on the earth is important because you can help others to know Him, thus bearing much fruit for Him. But as much as you love working for His kingdom on earth, you find the longer you follow Him the stronger your yearning to be with Him in heaven becomes.

Kingdom-Minded

Paul wrote to the Philippian church about the frustration of his longing: the conflict of the interests of his heart and the reasoning of his mind. He told them, "To live is Christ and to die is gain" (Philippians 1:21). He was truly torn. Torn between his desire to live and remain on this earth to *serve* Christ, and his desire *to be with* Christ.

He continued, "If I am to go on living in the body, this will mean fruitful labor for me. Yet what shall I choose? I do not know! I am torn between the two: I desire to depart and be with Christ, which is better by far; but it is more necessary for you that I remain in the body" (Philippians 1:22-24).

He had been so fashioned into God's heart that he was charged with a deep longing to be with Him in heaven. He wanted to truly be one with the One he loved, and yet it was for Him that he remained on earth. To serve His cause and build His beloved church, Paul had to stay here.

While serving Christ in this earthly realm, Paul knew that his citizenship was in heaven, though his kingdom purpose was in this world. His thoughts were not focused on what he could gain for this life. He knew that the real prize was in living this life as an investment for the eternal kingdom.

"Store your treasures in heaven, where moths and rust cannot destroy, and thieves do not break in and steal. Wherever your treasure is, there the desires of your heart will also be" (Matthew 6:20-21 NLT). He was kingdom-minded; his mind was set on investing in the joys of the eternal kingdom of God.

Jesus is calling you to cast off the worries and cares of this world in order to experience more of Him. God has so much more for you. He has even greater levels of His presence to share with you, but to experience it all you must free yourself from the entanglements that capture your heart. He's asking you to choose: Will you let the temporal distractions of this world keep you from Him? Or will you engage in a profound heavenly romance that will last through eternity.

He wants you to live a God-FILLED life – completely surrendered to Him, as a seed sown into this world. Live a God-filled life of delight in your Beloved that will truly catch fire and consume those around you with the revival fires of heaven waiting to be let loose on the earth.

More of Him

Years ago, during a time of prayer with a group of Christians at my church, I was overcome by feelings of remorse for myself and the church, and I wept uncontrollably. I felt the need to repent for my lack of focused devotion to Him, because I saw there was so much more of Him to experience – so much more He wanted desperately for us to experience.

I could barely catch my breath as I saw how compromise weakens us and our relationship with God is hindered by our disobedience. We have endangered our relationship with Him by seeking the approval of man. We have only accepted His lordship to varying degrees, yet the Word says, "If you want to be a friend of the world, you make yourself an enemy of God" (James 4:4 NLT).

Like Peter, I feel as though I would rather die than betray Him (see Matthew 26:33-35), but it is so easy to fall back into our man-pleasing ways and let our passion for Him dwindle because we long for acceptance. But by endeavoring to appease man, we have, to a degree, rejected our First Love and become vulnerable to feelings of indifference toward Him.

When I've endured accusation from misunderstanding it has, at those times, caused a fear of being misunderstood to develop in me. But then I realized that being understood is really unimportant and sometimes impossible. I realized that in this life, man's approval means very little and heaven's opinion of me matters much more. I did not want to betray my Lord in the process of trying to preserve myself.

This life holds many traps that can entangle and lead you away from your Lord. Indeed, He is calling you to live a radical life, making room for ALL of Him, not a slightly modified life that sort of fits your calling. Every day you live, you are asked to make a choice; every day you choose Him, the more you will want of Him – He is an insatiable, unquenchable hunger. And in following Him you will experience joy you never considered possible.

"Follow Hard After Me!" *A Vision*

The Lord showed me a vision of Jesus and myself walking briskly through a heavily wooded area. We traveled for some time, He in front and I behind. I knew He was taking me somewhere, that we had a destination. He told me to follow hard after Him. I repeated His words to Him to show Him that I understood what He meant, but neglected the word "hard." He corrected me, "Follow *hard* after me."

With His hand in mine we moved quickly through the woods. Many times branches slapped me in the face, but I kept following Him. Occasionally, we met people as we walked; some encouraged us while others hurled insults at us, but we kept walking.

At one point, I looked down and realized we had been walking on a narrow log which was no more than a foot wide. Below us lay a very deep ravine. I couldn't believe we had been walking so fast on what turned out to be a very perilous passageway. But Jesus seemed confident of where and how we traveled, so I grasped His hand even tighter.

We continued walking and, on occasion, we met people who would try to convince us that we were going the wrong way. When they found they could not deter us, they started to throw things at us. This made me mad, so I turned and started yelling at them. However, my yelling back seemed to increase their attack against us, as they pelted me even more with rocks and sticks.

Because I had stopped following Jesus in order to scream at our attackers, my hand had slipped from His without my realizing it, and He had disappeared out of sight. Instantly, terror struck me as I found myself on the narrow log with miles of open air below me that stretched to a rocky ravine.

I dropped to my knees, too afraid to journey on and too terrified to go back. I closed my eyes, hid my face in my knees and wept.

Suddenly, I felt a hand on my shoulder... it was Jesus. He didn't scold me. He very tenderly said, "Come on, get up, we've *got* to keep moving." He reminded me of His command to *follow hard after Him*, and so we started out again.

In the distance I saw a clearing where a river flowed. It glistened with the light from the sun. He said, "We'll stop there and rest a while." The journey seemed easier knowing there was a place to rest ahead of us.

As we arrived at the river, we took off our shoes and put our feet in the water. I was so tired, I just wanted to lie down and sleep, but Jesus made me eat a lunch He had prepared for us. After the meal, we lay near the bank of the river while the sun warmed us. It was really very nice.

It was then we met some people at the river's edge who began to flatter me. They wanted me to stay with them and help them; they told me that I was "just what they needed!" The temptation to stay with them was very strong because I was tired of traveling. I wanted to settle down. It felt good to be needed by them, but the Lord quickly pulled me away from them. As He did, I saw that they were wearing costumes and masks. They were not people at all, but were wolves in sheep's clothing.

I shuddered when I thought of how close I had been to staying with them. I determined in my heart not to follow my own reasoning, but to trust in His.

We continued our journey by walking along the bank of the river; it was very difficult. The banks were covered in jagged rocks and we were moving very fast. My ankles burned from all the twisting and turning the rocks caused.

After awhile, our difficult journey became monotonous and my mind began to wander. I thought of all I had endured on this journey and began to feel sorry for myself because of the insults I had endured.

Then, I remembered something that I had asked the Lord for a long time ago, which He had not given to me. I started to get mad at Jesus. As my temper mounted, I stopped and withdrew my hand from His. He turned and asked, "What's wrong?"

"Jesus," I said, feeling sorry for myself, "You didn't give me what I asked You for ... do You remember?"

"Yes," He replied.

I was convinced that I was in the right this time. "I really need that!" I declared.

He didn't get mad or annoyed with me, He just stroked my hair and said, "You don't need that right now, honey. It would only slow you down."

Instantly my heart was at peace. As sure as I had been that I needed it, I was now even more sure that *He* was right. *I knew now that I needed to stay focused on my journey ... to stay focused on Him.*

We continued on our way for a very long time, with fewer interruptions now because I had determined in my heart to follow *hard* after Him. I was beginning to understand more about Jesus, and I was learning what to expect from our journey together.

As we walked, the sky turned to a wonderful emerald blue and the trees became more and more beautiful.

The air was warm and filled with fragrance. Jesus walked much slower now, not quite as hurried. I knew we must be nearing the end of our journey.

We walked into a clearing where the grass was plush and green. I knew that where we were was a *secret place*. It was extraordinarily beautiful, peaceful and quiet. Giant willow trees hung like a picture frame over a gazebo by a gentle stream. Flowers filled the air with their scent. I felt I was home.

We sat down at the table where a delightful meal was prepared for us. We laughed together as we ate and talked of our journey and how beautiful the garden was. I was so happy to be with Him in this place.

Jesus continued to surprise me with wonderful fruit and all my favorite desserts. Everything tasted better than ever before; it was filling and satisfying. With every bite, I was filled more and more with His love, and the strain of my journey faded away. As we laughed and ate, I felt that I would be content to stay in this wonderful place with Him forever. I felt so refreshed.

Suddenly, heavenly saints robed in white appeared all around us as though they had always been there, but I had been unable to see them. They approached our table with great joy and carried gifts for me in their arms.

Jesus spoke, "These gifts are from Me. They are your reward for your dangerous journey." He beamed with joy at my surprise. "I love presents!" I exclaimed. I was so excited. They were wrapped so beautifully. I couldn't wait to open them.

The first present contained a small crown – I was stunned by its elegance. I took it out of its box and placed it on my head; everyone agreed it suited me perfectly. The second box contained a robe, which was red, trimmed in white. I was in awe of the look and feel of it. I slowly ran my hand down it, admiring the feel of the fine fabric. I started to cry at the thought of what this robe must have cost Him, and it was all for me.

I began to realize then, as if for the first time, just how much He really loved me. I looked deep into His eyes and said gratefully, "Thank You."

He smiled an understanding smile but then laughed, saying, "Put it on!"

I put on the robe and danced around to show everyone. They laughed and applauded with great joy.

As I danced I realized that my shoes were all of a sudden elegant slippers. They were not the worn out leather boots I had on during my journey, but beautiful silver slippers. I had not even noticed the change, and the Lord laughed with great delight at my shock.

Oh, how He laughed!

There was more laughing and dancing, talking and crying.

Then, secretly the Lord pulled a small box out of His robe and said quietly, "I have one more present for you."

I opened this gift with great reverence; I knew it must be something very special. As I opened the package and lifted the lid on the small box, I was amazed at what I saw. In this small thin box, with no elaborate trimmings, was His beating heart!

I gasped!

"I am giving you My heart, child, please use it well," He said. "I am sending you to where your journey began and you will need all that I have given you here.

"The harvest is plentiful, but the laborers are few, so I am sending you among the wolves to gather my sheep to Me. You must protect them. But, I have no fear in sending you, because you have all that you need ... you have gained it by following Me!"

He stood for the first time since we had arrived and, with great satisfaction at a job well done, He motioned to a small boat in the stream nearby. With help from the saints, we loaded my provisions into the boat.

Jesus unhooked the boat from its shoring and gave it a gentle shove out into the stream. I waved goodbye and blew Him a kiss, but could not take my eyes off Him; I wanted so badly to stay with Him in that beautiful place.

I did not know where my journey would lead me next, but I was not afraid. I knew that He was with me, guiding and protecting. He was my gentle Savior, sending me to battle with all I would ever need. I would not lack.

I then realized our journey had not ended in this place: it had only just begun!

Dearly loved of heaven, let your passionate love for Him ignite the world!

5

Heaven's Song

IMAGINE WITH ME a great multitude of people so immense you cannot see the end of it. You find yourself standing in the middle of this glorious, vast assembly, and as you look through the crowd you see that miles before you stands a magnificent throne.

The One sitting on the throne is radiant, with a brilliant, piercing light reflected like the facets of hundreds of gemstones all casting a different hue into the atmosphere. In front of the throne a shiny sea of glass sparkles like crystal.

You feel pulses of glory emanating from Him as they flow right through you, becoming more and more substantial. In them you feel glorified life – faith, joy, and love. Surge after surge, they rush through you until you are completely captivated by His presence and your entire physical body is enveloped by His glory.

Surrounding the great throne are twenty-four thrones for twenty-four elders wearing lavish crowns on their heads, clothed in white robes that seemed to flow into the river of glory that surges from Him who is seated on the throne. The effect of His glory is obvious on the faces of the elders as His overwhelming presence washes through them.

A hush falls over the crowd and you sense a heavy feeling of heightened expectation fill the room as every eye turns to the throne. People listen silently. You hear only the hushed breathing from the crowd.

Suddenly, intense thunderclaps fracture the air and lightning bursts out from the throne, pulsating with power. With it come heavy waves of glory that crash against you like a massive swell of energy. You feel as though you are in a giant womb feeling the vibration of your mother's heartbeat pulsating through you. You are shaken to your core again and again as you feel God's heart pounding through you.

Slowly in the distance before you, near the throne, you hear a sound rise ... a quiet, gentle sound. And as you look intently off in the distance, you realize the sound you hear is ascending from four beings surrounding the throne of God.

At the center, on each side of the throne, stand four living beings – they are frightful and strange in appearance, with eyes all over their bodies. One is like a lion, the second like an ox, the third has the face like a man, and the last is like an eagle in flight (see Revelation 4:7). And the song they sing is *heaven's song*: Holy, holy, holy is the Lord God, the Almighty – the One who always was, who is, and who is still to come.

As the living beings worship the Enthroned of heaven, the twenty-four elders, overflowing with love for Him, remove their crowns. Laying them before Him, they fall down and lie prostrate before Him, worshipping Him who lives forever and ever.

As they worship Him they proclaim:
"You are worthy, O Lord our God,
to receive glory and honor and power.
For you created all things,
and they exist because you created what you
pleased."   —Revelation 4:2-11 NLT

While the song builds in intensity, every heart in the room is overwhelmed with emotion as it fills them, and each individual joins with the elders as with one voice – filling the atmosphere with passionate praise.

Countless numbers stand in this sacred room, each person filled to overflowing with the glory of God. He is saturating every soul, and now all are one with Him and filled with His holy love.

As you stand there, in the middle of the awe and majesty, you are filled with such overwhelming love.

You struggle and even yearn for a way to express it. You long to give Him your whole heart, keeping nothing from Him, giving Him everything so you can express your love toward Him.

To lie at His feet is an expression of honor to display your overwhelming awe and love is your foremost desire. But what do you have to express your love? As you contemplate all of this, you realize you too have a crown of great price. Your crown represents the honor and love your Father has given you – your authority and your relationship with Him.

Your worship unfolds as a tender surrender of all you are – your crown you give willingly. And you lay at His feet every honor you've received – that is your privileged worship to Him. To give to Him what is dear to you out of the depth of a heart brimming with affection for Him. In essence, you surrender all you are to Him and say, "Let all that I am praise the Lord" (Psalm 146:1 NLT).

The worship He most desires, and what He's worked so hard and sacrificed so much to save, is you. Your love is what He longs for more than anything, because you *are* worship to Him.

He wanted you; He wanted to love you up close. The God of heaven who dwells in glory, who is continually worshipped, reached down and rescued you, called you by His name and clothed you with His glory to make you His own.

The fact that He wants you so desperately is reason enough to worship Him every time you take a breath. And every morning when you open your eyes, He is with you waiting to share the day with you. This is the One you worship.

Your worship is one of the most important activities in heaven and earth; the throngs of heaven await your expression of love for your Beloved. He wants you to know He loves it when you worship Him, even when you just sit and think about Him. And when you speak out the words the Spirit has placed in your heart, you captivate the attention of heaven.

All of heaven stops and listens as you declare what they all feel so tenderly; it ignites the praise of heaven. In an uproarious thunder of praise for Him, all of heaven combines with yours, joining in your song. The awesome praise lifts His glory higher and higher as it catapults to the roar of an angel-filled sky.

That is the power of your words, dear one. Let nothing stop your song. Heaven is waiting to hear you sing *its song*, the song of heaven.

His Response

Now, imagine yourself in an anointed worship service. The band is playing passionate, explosive music. The congregation surrounding you is worshipping and engaging. And you are caught up in the Spirit as you give

praise to God. In spirit and in truth you declare His great-
ness and your love for Him. Why? Because He is worthy!

He deserves praise, and you love to show Him that
you know He is worthy. You long to give Him the praise
due His name. It doesn't matter who's around you or
what they are doing, you give Him praise and you don't
care what others think. Your only thought is for Him,
and nothing will hold you back from flooding heaven
with your passionate worship.

It doesn't matter what your personal life is like, or
what difficulties you're dealing with. You know worship
isn't just a response to the blessings God's given you –
your love for Him is unconditional regardless of any circumstance in your life. You may feel broken and raw,
hurting and desperate, but He is worthy and you love
Him. Your hands stretch out toward heaven as far as you
can reach them. Waving them like a banner, you practi-
cally see Him now on His throne as you sing your song
personally to Him; face-to-face, you cry out praise to Him.

How do you think He reacts to your praise?

He wants you to think about how your love and praise
affects Him, because He is indeed soaking it all in. When
you worship Him, He closes His eyes slowly, leans His
head back, and breathes deeply. He starts to smile and is
flooded with emotion at the same time. He is soon overwhelmed and filled with love and gratitude. He reaches
His hand to His heart and begins to weep – He is undone.

That is what your worship means to Him.

As heaven looks on, the Almighty Lord of all is deeply touched by your declaration of love. All in heaven are deeply moved as they watch Him. Silence fills heaven. Then, quietly and respectfully, they begin to join the earth. Singing slowly and very quietly so as not to drown out earth's praise, but with a quiet echoing response, they close their eyes, still listening intently to the earth singing heaven's song.

Brimming with emotion, they begin to flow in response to the release in His heart, and they give in to their urge to roar with His praise. Heaven and earth join as one – hearts burning, as their desire for Him heightens. Now no words can comprise their hearts' passion, and a glorious thunderous response in heaven gives way to riotous praise, uncapping the glory-wells of heaven.

When His heart is filled with your praise, His glorious presence rushes to you and He grabs your hand as if to say, "Walk with me!" You are both caught up in heaven's song as He unfurls waves of His presence over you again and again. Unraveling your heart, He releases you to enjoy Him. His love melts your pain, drawing you to Himself. He finds you – His beloved lost lamb.

Beloved, there are many things you *do* for God that you may not realize He receives as worship. Your worship is so incredibly precious to Him; He listens and holds each word you speak close to His heart. He loves

it so much because it brings you closer to Him, and you
are what He wants.

> But an hour is coming, and now is, when the true
> worshipers will worship the Father in spirit and
> truth; for such people the Father seeks to be his
> worshipers.   —John 4:23 NASB

6

An Army of Glory

YOU DON'T HAVE to wait to be in heaven to experience God's glory! God wants to make you a representative of His power to bring heaven to earth. God wants you to encounter Him and experience His glory on earth, for you are a portal for the power of heaven to embrace the earth, releasing His glory to a very needy world.

God has shaped you and prepared you for this hour and for this day, to be a part of His last day army of glory. He wants to infuse you with His glory and make you a radiant beacon of light empowered by Him to illuminate the world around you.

The darkness of the world is increasing at an incredible rate, and many are crying out to God for help. However, His plan for illuminating the darkness is to send His children as lights all over the world. As darkness increases, His children become even more radiant in contrast.

The Lord showed me a glimpse of His incredible last day army of glory; I saw God's children filled with Him. I saw Him literally impart Himself into each individual and as He did, they were transformed. They were not only radiant in the darkness but also seemed alien to the rest of the world around them in their countenance and behavior. They were indifferent to the things that seemed to compel the world. Not driven by selfish desires, their only thoughts were for God's purposes to be executed on earth, and this empowered them with incredible joy.

In the vision, the earth was indeed in a truly darkened condition, yet God had established His people all over the world. Standing firm with quiet peace, they emitted incredible strength and confidence. They radiated immense peace when all around them was chaos and fear. The peace they carried was a glorious beacon of hope to the world and it gave them great influence and authority.

I felt they easily represented the Scripture, "Each one of you will put to flight a thousand of the enemy, for the Lord your God fights for you" (Joshua 23:10 NLT).

They were truly an army of great strength. Their strength lay in purposing to live only for the Lord's kingdom. They were filled with Him and purposed for God to be glorified in and through their lives, no matter the personal sacrifice required.

In fact, they didn't even recognize their sacrifices as being such; indeed, they viewed the sacrifices they made as gifts God had given to them. The pleasure they felt in Him needing them was an incredible blessing. They longed to be a blessing to Him, because He had rescued them and loved them when they felt unlovable – such was their appreciation of His love for them.

Through the blessing of their Christ-centered lives, they worked together in one accord, so much so that most of the time they would not need words to communicate with one another. They perceived by His Spirit what was needed.

I saw them as being one straight line of warriors; the rank of the soldiers in this army seemed inconsequential. They shared equally the roles of leadership, so no one would be overtaxed by bearing the burden alone. When one leader would need a rest, someone equally qualified would take their place.

It was unimportant to them who led, as they moved as one with no thoughts of competition or betrayal – to get more for themselves – but were very pleased to give help and encouragement to their comrades. Their minds, bodies and actions were filled with His radiant glory and they were therefore free to work with each other with complete trust and reliance.

As God dispersed them around the globe, they continued to be connected to one another through His

Spirit. Wherever they were sent they reigned with significant authority that has yet only to be seen in Christ. They were truly God's sons and daughters and loved each other with an indescribably deep love. They were bound together as if they were the same person, feeling each other's joys and pains as though they were their own.

They sacrificed their lives, their agendas and desires all to joyously embrace God's plans for them. They were numb to the things of this world as though they were already dead, yet lived still to display the glory of God on earth. They were the perfect depiction of Revelation 12:11, "They loved not their life even unto death" (ASV). Inside each of them I sensed a deep yearning to be with the Lamb of God in His glory, yet they valued their time on earth to fulfill the purposes of the kingdom.

The Enemies of Light

Some on earth, however, did not appreciate the light these saints radiated. They loved the darkness and saw anyone with His light as a violent threat against themselves and all they valued. They would do and say anything they could to deter others from following those who radiated the light, even to the point of trying to destroy them.

As those caught in darkness tried to expel the army of God, it seemed as though they would have their way. There were many more who were caught in the grip of the enemy than the number of those who held His light, and it looked like only a matter of time until the enemy would consume them. Yet they resisted them, not in anger but in love. They pitied those who would come against them; and hungered for them to receive the love of Christ.

Seemingly defenseless, they stood before a massive army of darkness yet did not waiver, standing firm. Closer and closer the chaotic violence came toward them. It wasn't until the enemy attacked them, however, that I saw an increase in the glory that pervaded them. With the glory came incredible authority over the darkness, and as they were assaulted they used their authority to lead those who came against them to Him who is light, revealing to the army of darkness an incredible sight.

Then, I saw the saints of God step aside, revealing to the lost the source of the light: a river filled with the glory of God. And that glorious river, teeming with the same power and light that emanated from the army of God, was a shocking sight in the midst of such great darkness.

Stopped by this breathtaking sight, some of those caught in darkness began to soften their hearts in His presence. They suddenly saw how passionately they were loved by God rather than hated as they had been told. As they allowed the love of God to penetrate them, I watched as the glory of the Lord washed through them, easily consuming the darkness that gripped them. It was a wonderful sight.

Time and again I saw them come to the river and be washed by His great love and grace; over and over as they came to attack, they found profound grace and forgiveness.

Still there were others, even at that incredible moment, who ran from the light seemingly to protect the very pain and darkness that gripped them. But the army of light had saved many from the grip of evil, giving them all reason to rejoice.

A Gateway for Eternity

As you surrender your life to God, you will see more and more that you truly are not of this world, but are influenced continually by the eternal world you belong to. You are changed by the glory of that realm and are continually and increasingly in its power. You begin to see yourself as the eternal being that you are, endued with the power and presence of His kingdom. You've encapsulated the heart of heaven and have brought heaven to earth. Indeed, you're now an ambassador of eternity – empowered by and teamed with all the children of heaven.

Compared to eternity, the life you're now living on earth is as short as a vapor or mist (see Psalm 39:5). So, the more you can embrace eternity in this life the more you will experience freedom from what holds this world captive. And the things of this world that seem so important begin to seem ridiculous by comparison. Indeed, they are not true reality but a façade to keep you from finding true joy, to keep you from experiencing true peace.

God's ways are so much higher than ours, but it is vital that we seek to know His ways and follow in them for the sake of our eternal souls and the destiny God has placed before us.

Just as the elders in heaven were consumed with worshipping God and pursuing what delighted Him, your life is made more abundant as you too pursue His glory, worshipping and delighting in Him. Your simple delight in Him will light the world.

Not Much Time

Our time on this earth is very short, and one of the greatest challenges of your life is how you choose to live the short time you have here. How will you use the time you have on earth?

People need to experience God's love, and truly, you may be the only "Jesus" some will ever know. God wants to use you to display His glory to the world. You are indeed a mighty beacon - a lighthouse in a dark and dangerous harbor. Your voice can release the life and power of heaven and transform those around you with a great awakening. You are a portal of heaven – the only hope the earth has to know of His great transforming power. *Literally, as you speak you release the power of heaven and change lives, breaking bondages of the lies of the enemy.*

So, speak! Speak out the glory of heaven! Open your mouth and transform this world. Let the lost know He is searching for them and longing to give them a brand new life.

Surrender this life, every moment, to Him to be lived *fully for Him*. Give Him all you are. There's not much time...

7

His Anticipated Bride

HEAVEN IS anticipating the awakening of the reigning bride of Christ and opening wide the doors to the government of heaven in preparation. For the first time in history we will see the realms of heaven touch earth, and we must match heaven's anticipation with our deliberate embrace of the authority and victory He's given us.

No longer should we allow shame to rule us. We must cast off passivity and realize our role as His bride. He has destined us to reign at His side and to care for the world as He would. His joy is for us to walk in His compassionate authority and dispel darkness, infusing it with light. As His church and His bride, it is our joy and responsibility to watch over and ignite the fires of revival growing on the earth.

The enemy has been busy harassing the body of Christ. He has tried to weigh us down with accusations and condemnation until we feel weak and incapable. But ask yourself, why has he done this? What is he afraid of? Why is he trying so hard to condemn us and convince us we are powerless? He lies because he is absolutely *terrified* of us. And the thought that we might actually discover just how powerful we are is horrifying to him. So, out of his fear of us, he hounds and harasses us.

What does the devil see in you that is so terrifying to him? He sees the righteousness of God (see 2 Corinthians 5:21) and untapped resources of the power of heaven. He knows the prophesy of Christ is looming before him and that at just the right moment, the church will indeed break forth in the power and authority of the Bridegroom, Jesus Christ!

The enemy is petrified of you, beloved. That's right. You may see yourself as insignificant but, believe me, you are what hell fears. When you stand to your feet, hell trembles. When you kneel to pray, it panics. And when you speak forth the truth of God in the authority of Christ, demons run screaming.

There are no little saints in the kingdom of God – no second-hand anointings. Each one of us plays an important role in the army of heaven. We must all do our part in fighting the enemy; we must take the ground where the Lord has placed us.

You *are* important to the kingdom of God. He needs you. God needs you to employ heaven's authority to govern this world; the power of God gains access to this earth through you. And through you His will is done on earth as it is in heaven (Matthew 6:10). *You are the door by which heaven touches earth!*

The love you have found in Him has the power to bring healing to the nations. The passionate love you share with your Lord cannot help but change the world – it is the greatest force on earth.

"Awaken, My Love" *A Vision of the Bride*

I saw in a vision a well-known evangelist. He was standing outside in the open on a platform before a sea of people. There were so many people, I could not see the end of them – the crowd went as far as I could see.

I watched him from behind as he faced the people. As he stood watching them, he began to comb his fingers through his hair and pull at it. Again and again he did this, clutching as if he were in anguish. He rocked back and forth in front of the people, overwhelmed by the vast number before him.

He looked at the people and threw up his hands to heaven, crying out to God in anguish, "Oh, God, there's too many people!" He was overwhelmed by the enormity of the need before him and the sight of so many souls hungering for Jesus. Searching the heavens, he screamed out in a loud voice, "Oh, Lord, awaken Your bride!"

Then the scene suddenly changed to a peaceful garden filled with rest and serenity. Lying on a bed in the middle of the garden was a captivating young woman clothed as a bride. Her hair was long and thick in a mass of perfect curls spread around her face and shoulders like a dark amber cloud. Her head was adorned with a simple white garland of flowers. She was absolutely the most beautiful bride I have ever seen – she took my breath away.

She lay like a portrait of peaceful tranquility on the cushioned bed, surrounded by the artistic garden that looked as if it had been fashioned to frame her. Her long thick lashes and full red lips rested still while her flowing white chiffon gown lay perfectly spread about her as she slept. Everything about her exuded purity – uncluttered beauty unlike anything I had ever seen.

Jesus entered the garden and approached her as she slept. As He gazed at her with awaited purpose, He bent down near her and touched her. He spoke, "Awaken, my love. It is time to awaken."

As she opened her eyes and sat up in her bed, Jesus stood back to watch her. She looked at Him with anticipation and stood to her feet. She looked searchingly at herself and straightened her dress, rightly placing her hair as if to dust off the remnants of her sleep. When she was quite certain she was ready, she looked at Him with eyes rich with adoration.

She ran to the Lord and threw her arms around His neck in playfulness, exuding sweet tender love for Him. How happy she was that He had awakened her. She hung her head back and gazed into His eyes, still clinging to Him. Her eyes spoke of the most pure innocent love.

She pulled back from Him with her eyes closed and face raised to His. She was completely filled with love for Him and her love was evident through the joy flooding her face. So full of a wonderful, indescribable love, she twirled in front of Him as if to enjoy the love she felt for Him. He laughed gleefully as He watched her dotingly.

She ran to embrace Him again. As they held each other, a bright, piercing light burst forth from inside her. Her body was soon encompassed completely by this incredible light. It exploded forth from her and filled the garden where they were. With eyes closed, head raised and arms outstretched, she stood illumined by the powerful light radiating from her.

Suddenly, coming from inside her, four silvery-white birds burst out of her stomach and flew in all directions. They surged upward in flight, soaring rapidly over the face of the earth, over mountains, oceans, cities and plains. They carried with them the same radiating light that emanated from the bride. Soon, the powerful life-filled light was saturating the globe.

The bride and her Bridegroom remained in the garden, adoring one another. He watched as she glowed with the light of His love. He wasn't surprised by her beauty but was completely pleased with her. He had always seen her beauty, and now she would captivate the world as she radiated His glory.

He knew fully that, at last, she was truly and completely His. He was assured that, in her eyes, there was no one else alive – she saw only Him. Likewise she was saturated in the confidence of His love for her. The knowledge of His passionate love for her made her illuminate His glory – a tangible expression of His love.

Dear saints, you are this woman, His bride. You are the bride of Christ. The world has yet to see your true inner beauty and to feel the waves of piercing glory that will burst forth from your love for Jesus.

The glory of God is made tangible to the world by the light of His love emanating through you. That love will spread to the farthest corners of the earth, canvassing it in His glory. Let Him purify you, beloved, to be made completely His, that you may be filled with Him.

"Awaken, my love, it is time to awaken."

Your Father is waiting for you to take hold of His extended hand so He can walk with you, making straight the paths – in an Eden-like relationship with you.

Let Him carry you; watch with utter amazement where He takes you. "Delight yourself in the Lord and He will give you the desires of your heart" (Psalm 37:4).

8

Belonging

Because I live, you will live also.

—John 14:19 NASB

WHEN I WAS barely sixteen years old, my mother and my ten-year-old brother were killed in an auto accident. My mother and I were very close. She was my best friend and I loved her more than anyone. She was the greatest Christian I have ever known; her faith was very genuine and transparent. She lived what she believed and she loved profoundly. Her life was never about herself but about blessing everyone around her. She lived to love. I loved her very much and still do.

For quite some time after my little brother died, I was plagued with dreams of trying to save him, only to wake up and realize he was gone. He was so much younger than my older brother and I, and before he died we were always looking out for him and taking care of him. So, when he was in trouble and needed us, it was a torment not to be able to help him.

Shortly after their deaths, my older brother, who was eighteen, left our home to live on his own. Soon after he left, my father moved to take a job in another city. I stayed in our home until I finished high school.

So, at sixteen, I was suddenly alone. My heart was broken, but I couldn't show it; I had no one I felt I could trust with that level of vulnerability. Keeping everything locked up inside, I was terribly lonely; I experienced times of emptiness, isolation and feelings of being forgotten. I fought feelings of depression and began to question my purpose.

It's difficult to explain, but with my entire family suddenly taken from me, I desperately wanted to belong to someone. I was envious of other families and wanted so much to feel again that sense of belonging I lost.

Although I had lost much of what I held most dear, I still had to live - to get up each morning and do *something*. But it was difficult to find my core purpose - the reason I was still here.

It was Jesus who rescued me from the loneliness I felt, and it was then that I truly began to know Him as I never had before. He became so much more to me, because I needed Him to be more. I was desperately needy. Because of fear, I didn't want to open myself up to needing any human person. So, God became my family and my everything.

He filled me with a deep sense of belonging – I belonged to Him and to His heavenly family. Suddenly, it was as if my whole world opened up, because I realized that the heavenly world (the world of heaven's kingdom) is more real than this life. As I learned more of Him, His family and His world, I found my purpose. He filled my emptiness and became my greatest joy.

Of course, there were times I wanted to rebel against Him, because I was so hurt. I was angry and yet, even though I rebelled against Him, though I wanted to hurt Him because I was hurting, He never left me. He continued to fill my broken heart with His supernatural love.

As a young woman, I danced, worshipped and rejoiced with Him alone in my house. I fell deeply in love with my heavenly Father. He became my family, my friend – always loving, never leaving. He gave me His life.

Though I was on my own, I was never really alone, as He was with me. I belonged to Him and He promised to never leave me. I found my "home" in Him; in Him I was finally at peace. He's the greatest joy of my life.

The Journey of a Seeking Heart

The Lord gave me this vision while I was studying the Song of Solomon. I saw a picture of "His darling," the bride of Christ, asleep in her bedroom as the Lord awakened her. She was pressed by God to chase after Him, to satisfy her need for Him, even at great cost.

In the end, she realized that all along He was leading her to Himself – to His secret place – a place of great glory and peace.

The Bride's Experience *A Vision*

The Lord came to the door of my room and called me to come to Him, but it was so late and I was tired. I was comfortable in my bed and didn't want to leave it. Yet as I thought of Him I felt a hunger for His presence growing in my heart. I decided to get up and spend time with Him, so I threw off the covers of my bed and ran to find something suitable to wear.

I was excited now to spend time with Him. I thought of a thousand things I wanted to share with Him. I felt anxious for His touch, to feel His strength and be comforted by it. As I fumbled through my wardrobe to find just the right clothes, I cried out to Him, "Wait, my Lord, one moment for me. I want to be just right for you!"

Hurriedly, I fingered through my jewels to find just the right beads. Finally ready to greet my King, I rushed to the door, barely able to grasp the handle for the excitement that mounted in my heart. I opened the door quickly, expecting to see His face. But my heart sank. He wasn't there!

My excitement quickly turned to disappointment and my desire to see Him to anxiety. I knew right away that I wouldn't be satisfied until I found where He had gone. Even though I wasn't dressed to go out in the night, I disregarded the chill in the air and plunged into the night to find Him.

My anxiety seemed to build as I hurried out. I started to feel desperate and I asked the watchmen of the city, "Where is He?" But they couldn't help me.

Suddenly, the thought sprang to my mind, "He's gone to His chamber." Quickly, I continued on through the dark city and found my way to His dwelling, but it was surrounded by 60 guards.

The sight of the guards terrified me. I didn't know what to do. Should I run away and hide or charge through them? Really, what choice did I have? Jesus was in there and I needed Him desperately; I decided to continue on.

Anxious but determined, I walked toward the 60 men guarding my Lord. I encountered the first and thought his blows would kill me, but I stayed on my feet and readied myself for another strike. One by one with painful blows they tried to deter me. Endlessly, I endured their attacks as they slashed at my face, hands and arms. I did my best to defend myself from them.

Unexpectedly, they stopped for a moment and looked at me questioningly. I turned my face to meet them with defiant resolve and, for a moment, I saw fear in their eyes. They realized finally that He was the One I belonged to, and they lowered their swords. They had thought they were protecting Him from me. They then realized that I belonged to Him. Indeed, He'd been expecting me, so they made way for me to pass.

I had made it through, but was bloodied, battered and bruised. The fight with the guards had made me unsuitable for Him. "How could He want me now?" I thought. My bracelets were gone, my gown was torn and drenched in blood, and the aroma of my perfume was swallowed up by the smell of sweat. But I couldn't let anything keep me from Him.

I opened the door to my King's chamber and entered timidly. Though I had been bloodied and wounded, His eyes rose to meet mine. My coming to Him didn't seem to surprise Him at all; He'd been waiting for me.

In the sight of His splendor, I felt ashamed of my appearance and lowered my gaze. But He beckoned me to come to Him. His invitation filled my heart with joy, but I cried, "I am unacceptable." Still He bid me, "Come!" I couldn't wait any longer, I ran to Him with arms outstretched and embraced Him.

In His embrace I found that I was no longer bloody, but radiant. The fighting passion in my spirit became a gown of splendor that adorned me, and my sweat, a costly fragrance. My fight had not made me unacceptable, but had prepared me for my King. I was made beautiful in my struggle and the blood that covered me became a gown to replicate His image. Though I was battered and worn, others saw only His reflection shining on me. Indeed, I was richly clothed in Him!

He wanted me clothed in His likeness, not in clothes of my own making. He dressed me in Himself, and I dwelt with Him in a palace of great splendor. Then I understood ... then I could see. He is *all*, and I was made complete in Him.

The Seeker

When Christ draws near to you and beckons you to come to Him, He does not always choose convenient times. Quite often they are the times you are busy or tired. However, once He comes to you, it's hard to resist Him until, finally, you leave the place you are comfortable in to search for Him. Suddenly you realize, indeed, He is all you want ... then you become the seeker.

Sometimes the Lord may seem far from you, but I assure you He is not. It's possible you've gotten distracted and need Him to bring you back to Himself. During those times God will develop a hunger in you for more of Him, more than you have previously experienced of Him. He wants to make you hungry enough for Him that you are willing to fight an army to get to Him, and even to fight through the pain we feel from those who may misunderstand our love for Him.

Your journey to find Him is what prepares you for Him, because He does not perceive things the way we do. The beauty of this world means little to Him, it's the beauty found in your heart that He treasures - that's the treasure He desires to uncover in you. Though you've been scarred by wounds, you find all you've endured on your journey has made you beautiful to Him. And through those scars you will radiate His glory.

Until you begin to disdain the comforts of this world *in comparison* to your desire for Him can you truly see or measure the value of the One you love. Only then do you see He is indeed the Pearl of Great Price, of greater value than anything you could possess on this earth.

His Invitation

God is moving in your heart to convey a hunger for Him. Why? *He has more of Himself to give you.* He must make you uncomfortable in what you've known so you will venture into the unknown, trusting Him to lead you. Then you will know Him as you have never known Him.

If there is, indeed, a cry of hunger in your heart, don't try to cover it up with busy Christian activities. Don't silence your heart! Learn from the trials that have magnified your hunger for Him. Answer His call.

God is calling you to a deep friendship with Him. Will you accept His invitation? Open your heart to Him today and say, "Yes."

9

Treasured Friend

He who dwells in the secret place of the Most
High, shall abide under the shadow of the
Almighty.   —Psalm 91:1 NKJV

THERE IS a secret place inside you where God loves
to dwell. It's a special place that He and you alone have
access to; it's your together place – a spiritual "honey-
moon" retreat. In this secret place, you can let your hair
down and be yourself with Him; He, in turn, will share
the thoughts of His heart with you.

The secret place is not a physical place, but it is
quite real and found hidden in your own heart. You
can physically (in the natural) be anywhere, surrounded
by crowds of people or all alone, and yet you can have
your focus directed only at Him. Quieting the sound
of the voices around you and the thoughts of your own

mind, you will suddenly find Him there waiting – you are instantly filled with His presence.

You can be busy at work, yet if you take just a moment to focus on Him, you will suddenly enter into His presence right where you are – in your secret place with Him. He is always there waiting for you – waiting to enjoy you – waiting to reveal Himself to you.

When you experience loneliness, even when surrounded by people, in the midst of "business as usual," He is the One calling you. That's because when you're feeling loneliness or emptiness, what you're truly longing for is oneness with Him.

He wants to be your God as much as He wants you for His own. He desires much more than to love you from a distance: He wants to hold you when you're sad, rejoice with you when you're victorious, and walk with you through life's journey (see Revelation 21:3).

Resting in His Presence

The prophet Samuel had never heard God speak until he spent time in His presence – it was there they developed their friendship.

Samuel lived apart from his family with the prophet Eli in the very temple where the Ark of God dwelt, exuding His presence. Even as a young boy, Samuel enjoyed being in God's presence and experiencing His power.

We see a picture of this in 1 Samuel 3:2-3, "One night Eli, who was almost blind by now, had gone to bed. The lamp of God had not yet gone out, *and Samuel was sleeping in the Tabernacle near the Ark of God*" (NLT emphasis added).

The lights were dim and the rooms were quiet; everyone else had gone to bed. But instead of going to sleep, Samuel went back into the temple to lie down near the Ark of God.

Although drawn to God at this point, "Samuel did not yet know the Lord: The word of the Lord had not yet been revealed to him" (1 Samuel 3:7). He'd never heard God speak, yet he was drawn to His presence.

During this time in Israel's history, none of the prophets were hearing from God. Eli's zeal for God had diminished and his relationship with Him cooled because he no longer enjoyed spending time with the Lord. So spiritually, the people were starving.

God needed Samuel. He needed someone who *wanted* to know Him, someone who could eventually speak for Him to His beloved people. But first, it was their relationship with each other that was vital; through it God's Spirit would be given fresh and vibrant to His people.

God needs you as well. He has anticipated a friendship with you that would radiate to the world. He needs you just like He needed Samuel, and He's calling you to Himself to develop the relationship that He's desired with you from the beginning of creation.

Your heavenly Father wants to build His kingdom in your heart, and the first step of that kingdom is Him. He wants to be the foundation you root everything in your life upon. Nothing else could withstand the glory of what He has planned for you. And it's only through His friendship that you will experience springs of living love well up in your life. He wants to make you a continual fountain of overwhelming realms of His glory. What He started with Samuel is *only* the beginning.

Wall of Love

In the spirit, God took me on a tour of His home in heaven and showed me an enormous hallway filled with pictures of His children. I could not see the end or the beginning of the wall. It was higher than I could see and was literally *filled* with pictures. That's all it was used for, just for pictures of His children, and He cherished every one of them.

As He showed me the wall, I could see He was proud to show it off, but sad, too. He said, "I have so many children that will not let me get close to them. They won't let me be a part of their lives. They will not let Me touch them. All I can do is put their pictures on this wall and look at them."

Beloved, God loves you more truly and completely than anyone on earth could ever love you, and all you need to do to receive His love is to embrace Him. He wants you to simply receive His offered friendship. He doesn't want your relationship with Him to be complicated by a lot of man-made rules about Him; come to Him simply as a child. It was as a child that Samuel made God his friend. He had no agenda when he went into the temple – Samuel, with pure child-like simplicity, just wanted to spend time in God's presence.

As adults, we have a tendency to complicate our relationship with God. The Lord showed me once just how He wanted me to come to Him. I was lying on my bed trying in desperation to touch God. I did not *feel* His presence and I felt frustrated, not enjoying my time spent with Him at all.

"Help me God!" I cried.

In walked my son, Cole, four years old at the time. He bobbled into the room with a goofy grin on his face. As he sidled up to the edge of the bed, he said in a very silly, childish voice, "Hi!" Then he walked away.

The Lord spoke to my heart at that moment, "That is how I want you to come to Me!"

I knew He was telling me to stop trying so hard to *get* into His presence and just *enjoy* Him as though He's already with me, because He is.

God wants you to be free from all of the self-made criteria of what you think He expects of you when you come to Him. He wants you to come to Him just as you are - a child with open arms of expectation, confident in His love for you - the very center of His attention.

God wants to be a part of even the simplest, most common tasks of your day, continually enjoying you. Through the common times with Him you will discover that He has entered into your thought life and is shining out through you - through the words you speak and the things you do. You begin to see the world the way He sees it, through the eyes of His thoughts.

Being God's Friend

Years ago, I went through a season when God shook everything in my life. One of those areas of shaking was my friendships. We moved to another state and distance caused my previous friendships to fizzle out.

I tried to make friends at our new home, but for the longest time I just couldn't click with anyone. I prayed for months for God to open the door to some good friendships, but nothing came of it.

I cried out to God, "Lord, what about me? Who will be my friend?"

He spoke beautifully into my spirit, "I will be your Friend; I want *you* to be My friend."

My eyes were suddenly opened to a treasure I'd possessed all along – the joy of being God's friend. I began to devote myself to a deeper friendship with God. I realized that, though I had been living as His servant, He was offering me much more. He wanted to give me a deep, abiding friendship. He was offering me *His* committed friendship, regardless of how I performed for Him.

There is no deeper friendship you can have than with your heavenly Father. He created you, knows you, understands you and loves you deeply. And when you mess up, He understands the reasons why and responds with insightful compassion.

Through your friendship with God, you develop a deeper understanding of who *you* really are. He wants you to come away from what you are familiar with – what you already know of Him – and seek Him afresh and anew. He wants you to discover new aspects of His character. Let Him open your eyes.

Samuel changed the world when he encountered God. What will you do when you encounter Him? I know it will be world changing!

10

Intimacy's Influence

DEAR ONE, you need never doubt God's acceptance of you. His faithfulness and commitment to you knows no limits. He longs to pour His grace and mercy on your wounded heart. And when you are hurting, understand that you can always run to Him, throw yourself at His feet and, baring your soul, be as truly miserable as you feel – He will not judge you.

He will not demand that you pull yourself together. No. He will get down on your level and let you cry it out in His arms until your hurt melts away in His presence – until He fills you again with His courage and strength that come when you feel so absolutely loved and accepted.

He welcomes and anticipates your needs; He wants to be the One you ask for help, no matter how minuscule or great your problems may seem. I know I can ask for help from a few of my friends if I need it, and they are happy to give it if they can. But some of my friends are so close to me that if I did not ask them for help when I needed it, they would be upset with me for *not* asking.

God ... is that kind of Friend.

The Lord is truly blessed when He's the One you run to with your pain or worries. Yes, He is thrilled and happy to be the One you seek after when you are in trouble. Once you've turned to Him, His heart is engaged in your need and He cannot possibly turn away. His heart won't let Him. It's simply impossible for Him to do so. He is influenced by the intimacy He's experienced with you. It's His relationship with you that makes it impossible for Him to turn away from you.

Fishing in Poofy Dresses

When I was a little girl, my parents lived and worked at a Christian camp in Minnesota; during the time we lived there, we were so poor that most all our clothing came from donations made to the camp.

In one such batch of donations came an old prom dress from the '50s. It was big, blue and poofy, but that old dress brought me a lot of joy. I wore it anytime I wasn't in school or church. I even slept in it. When I wasn't wearing it, I carried it with me. To a girl who had almost nothing, it became a priceless treasure.

One day I brought it with me when my older brother Danny and I went fishing with our friends. I'd played with it by the lake for some time, then laid it down on the dock and went back to fishing with my friends. I was busy and not paying attention to it, and when my back was turned the wind picked up the dress and blew it into the lake.

By the time I noticed it, it was quickly sinking into the dark murky brown water. I screamed for help because I was not a good swimmer. I couldn't go after it myself. And I watched as my precious dress sank out of view and down to the bottom of the lake. There was nothing I could do about it.

I turned to my friends for help and they ridiculed my panic. "It's just a stupid dress," they said. I knew they were right, but it was *my* stupid dress and it meant a lot to me. None of my friends would help me; they just stood there and watched it sink. I started to cry.

My brother stood there with our friends, watching the dress sink. But then he turned to me and saw me crying; I saw his head drop. He didn't want to jump into the lake with all his clothes on, in front of his friends, to save my dumb old dress, but he loved me. He thought my dress was stupid and he hated that I drug it around everywhere with us, but he loved me. And I was crying.

He heaved a sigh and jumped in the lake. Yes, he swam out and saved that dumb old dress. Just for me.

Because he was my brother and he loved me. My tears and my panic influenced him, but it was our relationship that obligated him to help me. And, dear friend, that is how God feels about you.

He cares about everything in your life, every situation, good or bad. He wants to be there to walk through it with you. And He will do whatever it takes to defend you. He wants the absolute best *for you*.

His love for you moves Him to change your situation; there's no greater friend. God has promised He will never leave you or forsake you (Hebrews 13:5); He will help you with things that may have no other value than that they concern you.

I Know You by Name

Moses' relationship with God was so profoundly intimate it empowered him with confidence to rely on God for help in any circumstance. God stayed close to Moses his entire life. He comforted him when he felt hurt or when he'd been rejected. God felt it keenly when Moses experienced feelings of inadequacy or when he was afraid. He was familiar with every aspect of Moses' life and loved Him deeply. God was intimately acquainted with Moses and knew him better than he knew himself.

Though Moses had a heart to rescue his people, he really had no way of grasping the scope of his true purpose on this earth. He was driven into the desert and was rebuilt by God's design. God needed a deliverer for His people, but their relationship became much more than that. In God, Moses found much more than his Lord, he found an incredible Friend.

Moses was confident in God's love for him and knew he meant more to Him than a mere servant. And because of their relationship, Moses did not shy away from influencing Him to help the people of Israel. When Moses cried out for mercy for them, how could God say no to him? It meant everything to God that Moses felt he could come directly to Him and boldly ask for His mercy.

Together, God and Moses delivered the people of Israel from their captors; but while Moses was walking with Him, an equally important event was taking place. A deep friendship was formed between them. Of all the people mentioned in the Bible, Moses is the one the Lord speaks of with great intimacy.

When Aaron and Miriam criticized Moses because of his wife, God was deeply offended by their behavior toward His friend and punished them for it. He spoke to them and said:

> Of all of my house, he is the one I trust. I speak to him face to face, clearly, not in riddles! He sees the Lord as he is. So why were you not afraid to criticize my servant Moses? —Numbers 12:7-8 NLT

Moses' feelings toward God were equally as intimate; their relationship was so profoundly personal that Moses wanted more to *know* God than he wanted blessings from Him. In Exodus 33:12-13 NLT, Moses said to God, "You have told me, 'I know you by name, and I look favorably on you.' If it is true that you look favorably on me, let me know your ways so I may understand you more fully and continue to enjoy your favor."

Drawing on the relationship they'd built together, Moses asked God a favor. And what, of all Moses could think to ask, did he want? What he wanted was more of Him; he wanted to know God more fully so he could serve Him better. It is no wonder God loved him so.

In Exodus 32, the people of Israel had sinned against God and He was deeply grieved because of their sin, so Moses interceded for them. The relationship had grown to such a degree that Moses was confident in God's affection for him and used it to help Israel – he used the influence he had with God to keep Him from destroying them. Moses spoke to God and said,

> What a terrible sin these people have committed. They have made gods of gold for themselves. But now, if you will only forgive their sin – but if not, *erase my name* from the record you have written!
> —Exodus 32:31-32 NLT, emphasis mine

Truly, God was influenced by Moses' devotion to Him and to the Israelites, so He agreed to Moses' request, and through Moses a nation was spared. He chose to find his delight, *not* in leading a nation but in *loving his God*. He wanted to do more than serve God, Moses wanted to know God and love Him – he built a friendship with Him. That friendship was so dear to God it turned His heart and saved a nation. "He said He would destroy them, had not Moses, His chosen one, stood in the breach before Him to keep His wrath from destroying them" (Psalm 106:23).

Confident in God

God desires to develop relationships with His children – it's His desire. And He seeks out those who *want Him*. Those who will relate to Him with childlike faith and trust; my mother was like that.

I don't think I've known anyone who had a relationship with God like she did. From the time I was very small, after everyone went to bed she stayed up late into the night to worship God. Always with her Bible in her lap, you would find her loving Him and treasuring the time she had with Him; it was their time together.

She enjoyed God and He enjoyed her – you could just tell. But as her daughter, it wasn't always easy being a child of a woman who was so close to Him, because God is a "tattletale." I can't tell you how many times one of us kids would be doing something we shouldn't be, and God would tell my mom about it.

[handwritten margin note: Are there ppls or nations or faiths or neighborhoods or families that need to I will stand in the gap for-]

One night, the night of the big high school basketball tournament, I was a cheerleader for our team. My older brother was a wrestler, and the wrestlers always drove to the basketball games together and hung out there. My brother was not living for God in those days and when he and his friends showed up at the tournament, they were all drunk. When the games were over, I tried to convince my brother not to go with the group he came with. I was worried about him riding with people who were so obviously intoxicated. I begged him to go home on the school bus with me, but he refused.

I worried and prayed all the way home that night. When I got home, I ran into the house and found mom in the living room. I ran to her and frantically told her, "Mom! We've got to pray for Dan! He's out with the wrestlers and they're drunk!" She said, in the sweetest calmest voice, "I know, God told me. He'll be all right," she assured me, and smiled her knowing smile. A few minutes later, my brother walked in the door of our house. All was well.

Whenever there was something to worry about, my mom refused to worry, she trusted. She wasn't trusting blindly, *she was confident in God because she knew Him.*

Knowing Him

Neither Moses nor my mother is any different from you. Their stories are unique because they wanted to know Him and experience intimate friendship with Him. That same intimacy is being offered to you right now. Jesus invites you to share your life with Him. He said, "If you abide in Me, the world is yours to rule and reign by My side." Indeed, He said, "If you abide in Me, and My words abide in you, ask whatever you wish, and it will be done for you" (John 15:7 NASB).

As you seek to know Him for who He is, and develop a *relationship* with Him, you will find He'll drench you in His great power and authority to reign with Him as His bride. You will reign, not in your own strength, but in the power and authority that belongs to you, beloved; you will, like Moses, have authority to influence your heavenly Father to intervene on behalf of those you love.

Intercession

Your words have great power in the supernatural realm as you abide in Christ. Instead of exhausting yourself by screaming at the mountains in your life, you will find that as you join yourself to Christ, you can speak the words in confidence and find your mountain crumbling before you. It is not your words the enemy fears, it is your relationship with Christ that terrifies him. As long as you abide in Him, you have all the power you need.

WOW

"As the branch cannot bear fruit of itself unless it abides in the vine, so neither can you unless you abide in Me" (John 15:4 NASB). The branch is an extension of the vine and has no purpose apart from being an

Wow. #5 an absolute.

extension of the vine – they work together as one. And as you remain in Christ (the Vine), you will experience a natural flow of His power working through you, resulting in much fruit.

As a Christian, it's impossible to produce lasting quality fruit apart from Christ. The fruit you produce flows directly from Him, because He chooses to flow through you. The quality of the fruit you bear is the evidence of your union with the Vine. That's why your relationship with Him needs to be your top priority, even above anything you do *for* Him.

God loves it when you bear fruit, but the enemy's trick is to get your focus off God and onto *trying* to produce fruit, which will leave you exhausted in your efforts to bear fruit apart from Him. Yet, abiding in Him and His strength, you will stay on course and press through to lasting victory and fruitfulness.

It is so easy to let the cares and concerns of life catch you off guard and eat away at your time spent with Him, but your relationship is a great treasure; it's the sustaining power for everything in your life and must come first. "Seek first His kingdom and His righteousness, and all these things [fruit] will be added to you" (Matthew 6:33 NASB, emphasis mine).

In any love relationship, time spent with the one you love is the foundation for the passion you feel for one another. Life can seem so urgent, even more pressing than spending time with your Lord. It is a battle to keep Him in His rightful place in your heart, but it's so essential that we fight for the One we love.

Beloved, your hunger to abide in Him daily and your desire to do His will as He asks *will* catapult you into your destiny in Him.

11

The Authority
of the Bride

ONE OF THE MOST powerful emotions is love, and there can be no true love without feeling emotion. God Himself is full of the pure emotions produced by love - He *is* love, and this Creator of love lives in us. His love for you is ferocious and passionate, so unlike the conception we have of His love on earth.

Some people believe that God's love is distant, void of emotion and subdued like the atmosphere you find in some churches, but He loves us with a much greater passion than most can even conceive of.

God has given so much to show you His love. The words, "For God so loved the world that He gave His only...Son" (John 3:16 NKJV) to save you will never have their true meaning until you are able to see them as a demonstration of His love for you. And He desires to continually express His love for you again and again.

God *is* love - He is passion - He is romance; the greatest romance in your life is what you and He will experience together. His faithful enduring passionate love for You, His bride, is the most powerful force in the universe.

Can you comprehend the power you generate through your shared intimacy with Him? Do you understand the influence you have with Him when you have touched His heart?

Just like with your earthly relationships, the more time you spend with the one you love, the greater your intimacy with them becomes; the greater the level of intimacy, the stronger their influence is in your life.

The marriage relationship can have the greatest level of intimacy of all earthly relationships. The Word of God says, "They become one flesh" (Genesis 2:24).

Usually when a woman marries a man she takes his name; with his name comes whatever honor or authority he has. I know in my own life, as my husband's name is one of honor, I am honored and treated respectfully by those who know him, because I am his wife. They may not know me personally, but because of the relationship I have with my husband, they treat me as they would him. And the Lord gives the same authority and honor to His bride.

A Proverbs 31 Bride

Proverbs 31 gives us an excellent example of how Jesus feels about you, His bride. It says, "Her husband can trust her" (v.11 NLT), and "She considers a field and buys it" (v.16)! She considers a field and buys it, because she knows her husband trusts her and she walks confidently in that trust. She has authority to do what she feels would bless her family. He has given her authority to manage their household because He has complete trust in her.   *Can I build that?*

As you abide in Christ you will find He has given you the same authority to rule the earth. And as you walk in Him, you carry His authority to speak into the heavenly realm. You can pray with confidence, knowing that you have authority to "call those things which do not exist as though they did" (Romans 4:17 NKJV). You as His bride are this world's only hope! Jesus gave His bride authority and then He commissioned us to preach the gospel and change the world for His sake.

Intimacy's Access

Authority represents God's trust – He gives authority to those He loves. In any solid human relationship, trust is the foundation. How awful not to be trusted by the ones you love – it is a huge part of the relationship we have with our friends. Love trusts, and God trusts His authority to you because He loves you. He has great joy when He sees you walking in the confidence of that knowledge.

As a sign of their oneness, many married couples share all their worldly goods, and in today's economy that usually means they have shared bank accounts. And both husband's and wife's names are on their account, giving them equal access to all their assets.

Jesus has put your name on His heavenly bank account! He has told all of heaven that whatever you ask in His name ... you shall have it! "[You] can come with bold confidence. And [you] will receive from him whatever [you] ask because [you] obey him and do the things that please him" (1 John 3:21-22 NLT, emphasis mine). By faith you have access to the blessings of Christ.

Saint, you need to start writing some spiritual checks! When you're His, you have access to all that is His. He gave you the key to death and hell; you need to use it. You can loot hell's domain with the authority of the Lamb. He said, "Ask of Me, and I will give you the nations" (Psalm 2:8 NKJV).

Through Christ, you have been given the authority of heaven with the power to affect this earth. This is your inheritance as the saints of Jesus Christ. Indeed, you are the bride of heaven, and <u>all of heaven awaits</u> <u>your command</u> to take up the mantle of Christ's authority and pursue the fullness of His resurrection power.

Heaven is waiting for you to mention a name, a situation or cause for them to fight for, or a demonic principality to destroy. When you do, the power of heaven rushes to answer your call!

I Love You Ferociously

I truly believe that if you see how much God really loves you, you will move mountains for Him. God's love for you is the fuel that empowers you to do great things for Him, and His love is the most powerful thing on earth. *No power in hell can stop you when God is on your side, and He is. If you will simply call out His name, He will run to your aid, leaping and bounding in ferocious love.*

During a time in my life of experiencing an exceptionally high level of demonic attack against me, I cried out to Jesus to reveal His love for me.

That night I had a dream: I was in a beautiful garden with many different flowers and trees. The sun was bright and beautiful. The garden was a glorious place to be, but I also saw three demons there. I watched them talking amongst themselves as they stood near the trees, until suddenly they saw me.

When they caught sight of me, they rushed toward me and were all over me in an instant. One demon lunged at my legs, grasping and clawing, trying to immobilize me. Another lunged at my chest, digging his claws into my arms. The third jumped on my back and wrapped his arms around my neck with a powerful grip, trying to choke the life from me.

As I slept, I was suddenly startled awake by the intensity of the dream. I sat up in bed with my eyes wide open. But even as I awoke, the dream continued like a movie before my eyes. I saw the three demon spirits attacking me and could feel on my physical body the effects of their attack.

Awake now in my room, I screamed out a rebuke in the name of Jesus. As I did, two of the demons flew off me, but the demon clinging to my neck remained. I could physically feel the demonic grip around my neck. I was horrified, yet my attention was drawn by something I saw in the distance running toward me at a tremendous rate of speed. It was an enormous lion.

By earthly standards this lion was abnormally large. He was the height of a tall horse but much broader, and his head was massive. As he bounded toward me, his mane flew out from his face as his paws struck the ground. He was incredibly beautiful and was indeed an awesome sight. He ran so fast that the hair on his body appeared to make waves like a wheat field blown by the wind as he leapt toward me.

The sight of the lion was more frightening to me than that of the demons. He was huge and charging at me with such tremendous speed that I was terrified. He was completely enraged, and his fury took my breath away.

His eyes were large and beautiful, but intense. He heaved and grunted as he galloped toward me, much like a warrior in the heat of battle. The fierceness in his eyes sent a shiver up my spine.

I began to brace myself against his inevitable strike. But then I caught another glimpse of his eyes and saw that they were not focused on me. I was not the target of his rage, but his focus was on the demon on my back. All of his anger was aimed at the demon that was clutching at my neck, whose grasp I could still physically feel around my neck.

As he approached at full charge, I felt the ground shudder as he landed again and again. As he came near to me, in one final burst of energy he leapt high in the air, opened his mouth wide and lunged toward me. In an instant, his mouth completely engulfed the demonic creature. Then, as quickly as the lion had appeared, he was gone.

The experience ended and I sat up in bed, completely awake. I was sweaty and out of breath. I looked to God and cried out to Him, "What was that?"

He spoke to me in the same fierceness I had seen in the lion in the vision, and said, "I love you ferociously!"

I knew that I had seen the ferociousness of God. Indeed, He was terrifying, but I had nothing to fear from Him because that terror was directed at my enemy, while His love enveloped me. My Jesus loves me, and the driving passionate love He feels for me is utterly terrifying to my enemies.

Jesus loves you ferociously, too, and your enemies shudder at the sight of Him! In Revelation 5:5, Jesus is described as the Lion of the tribe of Judah. He is truly awesome. He is our God and He is on our side. And He is driven by an all-consuming passion for intimacy with you. As His bride and as His friend, you have great influence with Him. He loves you and will move mountains for you. His love for you and your love for Him can win the world.

12

Freedom in Christ

MANY YEARS AGO, when I was a young woman, I found myself in a very legalistic church. While attending this church, I looked around at this small group of people and was overwhelmed with sadness because I suddenly realized that many of the people there were not trusting in Jesus to save them.

The enemy had led them to believe they had found salvation by relying on their own righteousness found in their adherence to the "laws" they had set up and taught. Quite sadly, they were held in bondage to their own judgments of who Christ was and became enslaved by their own assessments of righteousness.

Having been born again through Christ, they unfortunately, without realizing it, had replaced His sacrifice on the cross for their sin with a set of religious regulations and duties. With the instillation of the "new"

Wow!

rules for salvation, they could not see the lack they had in their spiritual lives. Without the ability to see their lack they, of course, would not be seeking true salvation. Their self-righteousness covered up their need for sanctification through Christ, for it is said, "Blessed are the poor in spirit, for theirs is the kingdom of heaven" (Matthew 5:3).

Naturally, I found that while I was with them, the freedom and joy I had found when I first knew Christ was slowly and methodically being stolen from me. I undoubtedly would have succumbed to their way of believing altogether if it were not for the teachings of my beautiful mother.

My Mother's Faith

My mother had a simple and loving faith in Jesus that, to a religious person, might have appeared childish and insignificant. But in reality, her love for Christ went much deeper than what most people experience. She lived in the joy of her Savior daily. She loved Him and He loved her; she was confident in her relationship with God and lived in great peace because of it.

When others would come and try to complicate her faith, she would brush aside their complex teachings with the grace and faith of a child. With a few simple words, she could stop the flow of these nonsensical teachers who acted as though they knew much more than she. I am sure they did believe they were helping her in trying to set her straight according to what they believed to be the truth, but she would just smile her loving smile, because she had something they had yet to realize: freedom in Christ!

She *knew* Jesus, and it was only through knowing Christ Himself that her freedom came. She did not know Him through head knowledge, she knew Jesus personally.

In most people's eyes, my mother was never anyone great. She was never a teacher, preacher or lecturer – she was simply a child of God. She *knew* her heavenly Father and therefore had the wisdom of heaven in her heart.

Before my mother died when I was only sixteen, she shared her Jesus with me. But, throughout the years as I pursued to know more of God, I got sidetracked from the simple, childlike faith she taught me. I had been trying much too hard to measure up to others' man-made rules about who I should be. It was only in remembering her and the love and genuineness of her faith that I found my way back into His arms.

Freedom Worth Fighting For

Paul said in Galatians 2:4-5, "Some so-called Christians ... sneaked in to spy on us and take away the freedom we have in Christ Jesus. They wanted to enslave us and force us to follow their Jewish regulations. But we refused to give in to them for a single moment. *We wanted to preserve the truth of the gospel message for you.*"

Paul and the other apostles were continually trying to re-establish the *simple* message of the Gospel to the Christians and protect them from the complicated deceptions of the enemy. He said plainly to them, "You are following a different way that pretends to be the Good News but is not the Good News at all. You are being fooled by those who deliberately twist the truth concerning Christ" (Galatians 1:6-7).

Back then, the apostles were the light that kept the twisted darkness of deception away. They fought to keep others free from the religious bondage that Christ had liberated them from. However, we know from church history that shortly after their deaths the church did succumb to the bondage of legalism and lost the freedom they had found in the simplicity of the Gospel message. In doing so, the world entered the darkest time in history, known as the Dark Ages.

Sadly, during this time, the very essence of Christ, which is love, was removed from Christianity and was replaced with stringent laws. The Father/child relationship that God longed to have with His beloved was stolen and replaced with a demanding tyrannical view of God more easily used to manipulate the people for unholy gain.

It remained oppressive until the truth of the Good News of Jesus Christ was recovered by many brave souls who fought for truth during the Reformation period. For some, it cost them their lives. And with the same passion they had in recovering the Good News, *you* must fight to keep the simplicity of your faith alive, defending the message of His love and mercy in your heart.

Your passionate defense of your First Love will be the guardian of your heart against the thieves of the enemy who want you to surrender the freedom and joy you've found in loving Him. The enemy seeks only to supplant it with a twisted gospel that complicates even the smallest truth and will inevitably lead you to a false reliance on your own self-righteousness, which is bondage.

Jesus alone is your deliverer and He is all you need. As you cling to your First Love, Jesus, your light shines and joy is revealed. The bondage of condemnation is shaken off you as you simply *enjoy* the romance you have with your First Love, and truly that is the image of Christ.

There is no "new gospel" or any religious dogma that supersedes what Christ has done for you on the cross. He alone carries the power of life for you. Indeed, Jesus *is* the key to your freedom. His love for you will unlock the chains of sin and condemnation, liberating you to enjoy Him more.

The Lord says to you, "Beloved, return to Me. Live in My love and let *Me* dispel all the shadows of the past.

Shake off the complexities of religion and return to the simplicity of living in My love." He loves you and just wants you to enjoy loving Him in return. If you will live in His love, He will transform the world through you.

Freedom in Trusting His Plans

Freedom is found in giving God control of your life, because He says, " 'For I know the plans I have for you,' declares the Lord, 'plans to prosper you and not to harm you, plans to give you hope and a future' " (Jeremiah 29:11).

Sometimes our *own* desires can cause bondage, but freedom comes from trusting that God is compelled by love to fulfill His plans for your life. They are, after all, *His plans* and His desire for you. You can trust Him because He does have your best interests in mind and will fulfill any promise He's given to you.

Beloved, you in turn relinquish the plan and promise to Him as a seed of faith and trust that He chooses to bless you, *to prosper you and NOT to harm you!* And when you trust Him, He will do "immeasurably more than all [you] ask or imagine" (Ephesians 3:20).

When God puts a desire in your heart, that desire is meant to draw you closer to Him; He wants to fulfill that desire within you. He wants to work with you to supply all that you need. It's a journey He cherishes. His joy increases as He watches you grow closer to Him through your struggles. He wants to accomplish much more for you than you can imagine; He wants to build a friend.

Leah prayed for years for her husband, Jacob, to love her. He had been tricked into marrying her and had always resented it (Genesis 29:16-29). She bore him son after son and still he would not love her. With each son, she prayed he would love her. Leah's heart's desire was for her husband's love, but in seeking God for her desire to be met she unexpectedly found an even greater treasure – a friendship with her heavenly Father. And in finding Him, she found her heart brimming with joy whether Jacob loved her or not.

She gave God her longing for Jacob's love and He gave her Himself. She could live without Jacob's love if she had to because she found out just how completely God loved her. And in His love her heart would soar even though her situation had not changed (Genesis 29:31-35).

"Delight yourself also in the Lord, and He shall give you the desires of your heart" (Psalm 37:4 NKJV). In Genesis 29:35 we see that Leah had found her delight in the Lord and her focus had changed. No longer did she wait to be happy. She surrendered her emptiness to God and He turned her heart's pain into sweet peace. And because she now lived in the freedom God gave her, her husband grew to treasure her love in return.

Power in Freedom

Years ago a pastor friend of mine was going through a very difficult time in his church and ministry. As he got up in his pulpit one Sunday, he found himself weighed down with heaviness and couldn't seem to shake it. He was unable to go on with his message, so he stood before us with his eyes closed. On the verge of tears, he asked all the children and the childlike in the audience to join him on stage.

In a spontaneous moment of reckless abandon, he told the worship team to start playing music and he had all the children dance on stage, but he did more than watch. In front of the whole church, he danced. He danced with the children until his heart was renewed and God's presence *filled* the place.

There is power in freedom! All of heaven treasures the freedom you walk in. When you dance, all heaven dances with you. When you delight yourself in Him, you, in turn, delight heaven.

Your enjoyment in God is priceless to Him. It is a treasure of untold riches, and God will protect it at all costs. He wants you to know Him as He is and allow Him the pleasure of knowing you as you are – freeing you to be who He made you to be.

He will not share your heart with the claims of respectability – He wants you and you alone; your heart, your mind, and your strength ... all that is you will be His to love and enjoy.

Don't let anyone take your enjoyment of God away from you. It will break His heart if you think you have to be miserable to please Him.

Return to your First Love. Live in Him and let the light of Christ dispel all darkness. Shake off the oppressive teachings of a man-made gospel and return to the simplicity of loving Jesus. He loves you; simply love Him back. Live in that love every day and watch your world be transformed.

13

The Promise
of His Presence

If You don't personally go with us, don't make us
leave this place.   —Exodus 33:15 NLT

IDEALLY, ONCE you've decided to live for God, you
sell out wholeheartedly, never turning aside or stumbling to find your way. But like Paul in Romans 7:14-15:

> We know that the law is spiritual; but I am
> unspiritual, sold as a slave to sin. I do not
> understand what I do. For what I want to do I do
> not do, but what I hate I do.

It's so easy to get distracted from living the God-
packed life we desire, and we find ourselves instead
wrestling with things that sidetrack us from Him.

It's difficult, even dangerous, living outside of God's plan for your life; it's a lifelong struggle to stay in the center of His will. It's important to continually renew your commitment to Him, putting Him back on the throne of your heart – making Him your all. God is so merciful and kind. He is filled with grace, so when you slip you can call out to Him to draw you to Him again, and you'll breathe in His fresh grace.

If You Don't Go, Don't Send Us

In Exodus 32-33, after everything God had done to deliver the Israelites from their oppression in Egypt, they doubted God and chose to worship a golden calf instead of Him. They even went so far as to declare the calf as their redeemer who'd brought them out of Egypt, instead of the God who loved and cared for them. Their betrayal crushed His heart, so He told the Israelites He would help them get to their Promised Land, but then He's finished with them.

> The Lord said to Moses, "Get going, you and the people you brought up from the land of Egypt. Go up to the land I swore to give to Abraham, Isaac, and Jacob. I told them, 'I will give this land to your descendants.' And I will send an angel before you to drive out the Canaanites, Amorites, Hittites, Perizzites, Hivites, and Jebusites. Go up

to this land that flows with milk and honey."

—Exodus 33:1-2

God told them He would give them all He'd promised them, but then He ended with this statement: "'But I will not travel among you, for you are a stubborn and rebellious people'" (Exodus 33:3 NLT).

After their sin, God in essence told the Israelites, I will send you to the Promised Land because I promised it to your ancestors, but *I* am not going with you. When the people heard the devastating words, they mourned the loss of His presence, "went into mourning and stopped wearing their jewelry and fine clothes" (Exodus 33:4).

Their mourning of His absence demonstrated to God how much He meant to them. They finally realized how much He meant to them, too, and they wanted His presence with them at all cost. They wanted Him for more than His miracles; they wanted Him because He was *their* God and they needed Him.

It's easy to start going your own way without recognizing it. When you find yourself in a muddle, you see how great your need of Him is and turn back to Him. What a treasure your return is to Him – when you come to Him again and give your heart to Him. When you realize your absolute need of Him you will not continue on without Him by your side. You want to show Him it's Him you want and not just what He can do for you.

Moses told the Lord in Exodus 33:15-16, "If you don't personally go with us, don't make us leave this place." Moses was saying he didn't want the Promised Land without God. His relationship with God meant more to him than the promises the Lord made to him.

Moses wanted God's *will* because He loved God and wanted to live for Him. We, too, must decide who we will serve and why. Will you continue on in your pursuit of what you think you want, even if it means missing God's perfect plan? Or will you determine in your heart not to take a step in any direction unless you know He is with you. True happiness will only be found in Him, and your relationship with Him is His number one priority.

We, as His body, need to realize that without God in our churches, they are just big empty buildings of no special significance. Cool, cutting-edge worship teams without His power possessing them only make a lot of noise. And speakers who speak only for themselves say nothing of any lasting value. But it is, indeed, His presence that makes the difference.

When He's with us, it is an awesome thing! It is God invading earth! In those moments, we should spend time just basking in and appreciating Him. Our churches should be a showplace to display the greatest romance the world has ever known – our love for Him and His for us. It's where we enjoy Him and He enjoys us – as we unite with others who've come to love Him as well.

Truly, a genuine seeker longs for the real presence of God no matter how He wishes to show up, no matter what He wants to do while He's here. One of the snares that can hinder your relationship is the idea that you always have to *do* something when you're with Him. Sometimes He just wants to sit with you and hold you or share something with you. And if you slow down, you will discover a great treasure you didn't know existed.

Our Reaction to His Presence

When Jesus came to visit Mary and Martha (see Luke 10:38-42), Martha wanted to *do* something for Him as she made preparations for a meal, but what He wanted was just *her*. All Mary wanted to do was to be with Him and sit with Him, enjoying His presence. Martha thought she knew what was pleasing to the Lord and demanded the Lord rebuke Mary for not helping her. However, the Lord disagreed and said, "My dear Martha, you are worried and upset over all these details! There is only *one thing* worth being concerned about. Mary has discovered it, and it will not be taken from her" (Matthew 10:41-42 NLT, emphasis mine).

Jesus took Peter, James and John up to a high mountain in Matthew 17:1-6 and was transformed by the glory of God. Moses and Elijah suddenly appeared before them and spoke to Jesus. Heaven literally opened before them, revealing Jesus' divinity. But poor Peter was so awestruck he didn't know how to respond to this incredible experience. He wanted to *do* something (Matthew 17:4).

Instead of being frozen in his tracks, collapsing to the ground and awestruck by the glory of God, he offered to build tabernacles for them. Well, what would you do? How would you respond to God's glory? It's difficult to know until it happens to you. Indeed, Peter was a doer, Martha was a doer, and God loves doers. But even doers have to learn to stop and enjoy Him, for there are times when God doesn't want us to *do* at all. He just wants us to *be* – to stand in awe and experience Him.

"Experience Me"

When I was young in the Lord, one time I had been going through a difficult time in our church, so I cried out to the Lord. As I lay on my bed that night, I sensed a strong, awesome presence enter my bedroom. I knew instantly I was in God's presence. I lay rigid on my bed, short of breath, not knowing what to expect.

Suddenly, I felt His presence touch me, and in wave after wave His incredible presence rolled over me again and again. I didn't know what to do. It was overwhelming. I didn't know how to react and I thought, "It is such an awesome thing to be in the Lord's presence;

He must have some amazing news to tell me or some important task for me to do."

As He continued to bathe me in His presence, I asked Him, "Lord, what do You want me to do?"

His reply sent my heart soaring. He said, "I just want you to experience Me."

God loved me so much He came to me in my little house so I could experience Him. I was never the same from that night on. That experience was the beginning of a craving in my spirit, a craving to experience Him for the rest of my life. I would experience Him on even greater levels in the future, but I will never forget that special night when He chose to reveal Himself to me.

14

Completely His

THE LORD has strategically placed His passionate lovers, His intimate friends, all over the world. I saw them in the spirit as spots of light on a globe, and the cry of their heart is, "More, Jesus!" And the more they cry, the more they receive, until they are drowning in uncontrollable love for Him.

Their passion for God is so true and genuine that, at times, those with a cynical mindset think it could not possibly be real. But as those who are suspicious begin to see the reality of the faith of His dear ones, a divine jealousy is birthed deep down inside their hearts. Without even realizing it, there is an emerging awakening in them as well: a cry for "more!"

As you sweetly surrender your life into His hands – as you are spilled out and poured at His feet, you can be certain that everything you are will be needed to strengthen His bride. The more you are purified, the greater your love for Him becomes, and the more beautiful a fragrance you become to Him and to those around you.

Only One Master

It's natural for the hidden agendas in your heart to surface and pressure you to want your own way. But if you follow those desires you become the master of your own heart and compromise your relationship with Him. "No one can serve two masters. Either you will hate the one and love the other, or you will be devoted to the one and despise the other" (Luke 16:13).

Giving God control of your destiny is scary, but risk-free; He loves you so much and has way better plans for you than you would have for yourself. You would be content with much less than He intends for you, but He sees your life in the light of eternity and knows what will best suit you and what will keep you close to Him. He has a place perfect for you. And living in His will is worth any cost.

What cost are you willing to pay to serve Him? Sometimes we think we don't have much to offer God. We devalue what we're doing for Him or think it is not "spiritual" enough, but all God asks from us is to obey Him. If He asks you to be a missionary, then you will be pleasing Him by doing that. But no matter what He asks you to be, you are still serving Him, and your work (all aspects of it) becomes an eternal work. God does not differentiate between the spiritual and the natural; it's all connected in His eyes. It's not about how much you give, but how much of *yourself* you give to Him. Will you give Him just enough, or your whole heart?

The widow in Mark 12:41-44 gave more than her rich counterparts, because she gave all she had to live on. The rich gave out of their surplus, but she out of her need. All God wants is *all* of you. Whether you are little or great, He just wants your heart.

Sometimes when I am caught up in the worries of life the Lord speaks one phrase to me and it settles my spirit instantly. He says, "Victoria, give Me your heart." I know what that means. At that moment, I'm not trusting Him with my whole heart.

If you want to serve Him alone, you have to give Him your all. Give Him your whole heart and watch Him turn your world upside down with His glorious victorious presence!

You will never be able to please everyone, but you can please God. And pleasing man is a trivial matter when compared to experiencing God in His glory.

Jesus was completely set on absolute obedience to God. Truly, He served the kingdom of heaven and not the kingdoms of this world. His obedience cost Him everything, but He gladly gave it all.

What a torment – to give your life to Christ yet slip back into the worries of life. How awful to live only half-way for the Lover of your soul. Jesus knew what torment double mindedness was when He said, "I know all the things you do, that you are neither hot nor cold. I wish that you were one or the other! But since you are like lukewarm water, neither hot nor cold, I will spit you out of my mouth!" (Revelation 3:15-16 NLT).

On the surface, that doesn't sound like He loves us at all. But, in reality, it is the *height* of His love for us. It is difficult for Him to hand us over to what He knows will only hurt us: *the fulfillment of our own desires.*

Like Peter discovered, when you place your desire for acceptance from people above your love and desire for Him, it's a great torment. It's paralyzing and you will never totally please either yourself or God. He understands the enemies of your destiny. It is only by letting you go, allowing you to serve your other master, and getting wounded by it that He may gain your heart entirely.

Surrendered Destiny

As He said to Peter, "Simon, Simon, behold, Satan has demanded permission to sift you like wheat; but I have prayed for you, that your faith may not fail; and you, when once you have turned again, strengthen your brothers" (Luke 22:31-32 NASB).

It was only by allowing Satan to sift Peter that God was able to use him to strengthen his brothers. He needed to be purged of all that was in his heart that would compromise his faith: his heart's hidden fears and desires. Jesus did not deliver Peter from his trial; He allowed him to go through it, praying for him all the while.

Peter wanted to give his all to Jesus, but he was paralyzed by his hidden fear of man. You may not realize it, but like Peter, *you* may have hidden idols in your heart. We all have a propensity toward our own desires, but anything that causes you to serve *self* will only hinder your ability to give Him your all. Laying it all down at His feet is the most freeing thing you'll ever do. You can trust Him to fulfill the desires of your heart in the best possible way, because He is completely motivated by His all-consuming love for you. He wants the absolute best for you and nothing less, but He will make sure you are prepared to handle it first.

The Blessing of Brokenness

To give yourself completely to God is the only way to have more of Him in your life. It is only when you are sifted or broken that you can fully open your heart to Him. Only then can you be completely His; therein lies the *blessing of brokenness*.

Yes, you will find blessing and even joy in brokenness when you undergo the sifting and purging of your heart as you surrender it to Christ. Surrendering everything to Him, keeping nothing from Him, is the only way to possess Him. Abraham gave God Isaac and received a nation and much more, and even received his son back through his obedience (see Genesis 22:9-11).

To the rich man in Mark 10:17-22, when he asked how he could better serve God, Jesus replied, "Go and sell all you possess and give to the poor" (NASB). Jesus wanted to know to what degree this man belonged to Him, by requiring "everything." Sadly, He found the man unable to let go of his identity rooted in the wealth around him. It was a test to see just how much he wanted Him, because God was unwilling to share him with the world.

God is asking the same of you today. He will not force you to want Him. He will not make you obey Him. But, in truly desiring Him from the depths of your heart, you open up a door to the most passionate purpose possible in this life. The greatest adventure life has to offer you is Jesus, as you walk through life's journey with Him and learn to love Him more.

Self-Justification or Humble Surrender

One day, I had a difficult time with one of my children. They were somewhat defiant and disrespectful to me. But what I especially didn't like in their behavior was their desire to stay in control. I tried to show them what they were doing wrong and how they were coming across, but it didn't work. So, the harder they pushed to show me they were right, the more determined I was to see a desired change in their attitude.

What did I want from them?

Surrender... full, absolute, complete and humble surrender. Their punishment became more restrictive until, at last, they humbled themself and submitted. It was really beautiful to see the change in their heart and sense the change in their spirit.

I said to God, "Wow! That must be how You feel when we finally let go of our 'need' to be right and be in control, and just let You have Your way with us."

It's human nature to either justify or condemn yourself when you've blown it, but God doesn't want you to do either, anymore than He wants you to rebel. True repentance is basically saying, "God, You're right and I'm wrong." There's no justification needed with Him because He already knows your heart thoroughly. He knows your heart much better than you do. You don't need to worry about how you appear to Him because He knows your heart and loves you anyway.

When relating to God, you don't have to be right, just real. He's on your side and only wants the best for you. Your Father has journeyed through life with you

and seen every hurt and pain. He will bless you for all
you've endured, and a part of that blessing is the heart
He is building in you – a heart that is strong and able to
bear up under the enemy's attacks against you.

He sees more correctly how you're feeling. He sees
straight through you to all that you really feel inside,
and why. He knows the wounds that cause you to react
the way you do, He knows what makes your heart ache.
That's why He targets the weak areas in your heart to
strengthen and heal.

Though at times you may feel you are unfairly chal-
lenged, believe me when I tell you it is because He
does love you greatly that He wants to bring you to a
place of healing. He wants to target the wounds in your
heart that have become bitter memories and walk you
through to see them the way He does. He wants you to
understand them in light of His kingdom and glory.

Thank God, He loves you enough to stand His
ground and keep you from ignoring the areas of your
heart that are hurt and need attention – to bring you to
a place of peace. Because of His love for you, He believes
for the best in you. God doesn't want to crush or annihilate you. His goal is to correct you in a way that will bring
you into a right relationship with Him so He can walk
with you like He walked with Adam and Eve in the Garden of Eden, because walking with you is God's "paradise" and it's the only place of abundant life for you.

It is His love for you that keeps Him believing and dreaming for your destiny. It's His longing for you that maintains His commitment to you. He doesn't want to dominate you. He's waiting for you to give yourself to Him in complete and beautiful surrender.

Let yourself relax in His arms. It's okay to be yourself with Him; He knows everything about you and loves you passionately.

15

Majestic God

AS I SAT alone in my room, I started thinking about God. Suddenly I felt a spiritual curtain pulled back and I could see into heaven's realm. I was absolutely taken aback and literally gasped. I saw our heavenly Father and He was overwhelming in His beauty and glory, but His glory encapsulated much more than Himself.

He was beautiful, overwhelmingly powerful, but what made Him so awe-inspiring was the robe He wore. It was a long ethereal robe flowing as though it were alive, made up of literally thousands and thousands of *people*. As He threw His arms open wide, I saw even more people in the sleeves of His garment. Looking closer, I saw the people in the robe had been so enveloped by His glory – so consumed and transformed by Him – they were actually blended into the fibers of His garment, creating a glory-filled robe He wore proudly.

As I watched, I saw the people in His robe illumi-
nated with incredible joy – they seemed lit up from
within. And He seemed so proud of them and happy to
show them to me. However, my physical body seemed
shocked by what I saw and it trembled in response. I was
frightened by the awe of Him and melted. As I continued to stare, I felt His sustaining power wash through
me and fill me with His love.

As I lay there, touched by the intensity of His amazing love, I felt the confines of my unbelief and doubt
begin to fade away, and then I just knew that with God
working through me there would be no dream I could
not realize – nothing He could not accomplish through
me. With His power in me, I was truly more than a
conqueror. *He* made me fearless. I was filled with joy.

Truly, He is breathtaking, even fearsome, buffered
only by His immense love. He chooses to make His
most treasured creation a showcase of His glory, and as
He inhabits His creation they become a part of Him –
reflecting His glory. Nothing in life makes Him more
proud than His dear children – His most precious creation. He values them all for their individual unique-
ness, but sewn together in oneness with Him they make
a stunning display of His creative majesty.

All of a sudden, He flooded my mind with two jour-
neys of thought: first, He is indeed awesome and to be

revered, respected and feared. And then, my need of Him is absolute.

He is everything the Bible claims He is and MUCH more. Yet He has chosen to call Himself our Father because He created us to be His family. He chose you to be His friend and desperately wants a relationship with you. He is the Almighty, holy God of the universe, with more majesty than can be imagined on this earth. And He loves you and chooses to make you His own.

He is your Father and you are His child. You belong to Him and you are immensely powerful when you are *in Him*. Immersed in Him, fear and regret cannot hold you. Though you may feel inadequate in yourself, you are mighty in God. And with His power working through you, you really do have the power to transform nations. He is great, and in Him *you* are made great.

In His presence all selfishness melts away, pride is irrelevant in the face of His glory. You are simply absorbed into Him and His glory, and you feel perfect liberty and wholeness, because in Him you have everything.

Desperate Need

As I watched Him, I felt He was insisting that I also see my desperate need of Him so I would stay close to Him. Indeed, it was very terrifying to see my complete dependency on Him. For, I felt the weight and reality of my sinfulness apart from Him – to be utterly lost except for Christ's sacrifice for me. I felt wretched in myself, as an excruciating pain shot through me when I realized the pain my sin caused Him.

Our salvation is not a light thing. It's an intensely miraculous event. God's pursuit of you is a marvel; His love for you is never more evident than in the Cross. It's the greatest act of love. Indeed, it is the single greatest love you will ever experience, as the almighty God and Creator pursues you and rescues you, restoring you to Himself.

Nothing pleases Him more than when you run to Him and throw yourself into His arms, receiving the awesome gift of salvation He's provided for you. He longs to rescue you and give you the gift of life with Him – to make you His heir.

As you go about your daily life, it is easy to forget that there will be a day of judgment for this world (Revelation 20:11-12). God knows we will all be judged whether we believe in Him or not. In reality, only He can clearly see just how great our need truly is. He has spared nothing to rescue you from the judgments of sin, and nothing in this life will matter more on that day.

WOW!

Your Father is crying out for you to fully receive His grace and let salvation have its completed work in you. It's crazy, but your fleshly nature is very tricky and will try desperately to convince you that your own goodness will save you. Yet, *self*-righteousness ("earned" right-ness) is a treacherous enemy seeking to negate Christ's sacrifice.

The truth is, "When we display our righteous deeds, they are nothing but filthy rags" (Isaiah 64:6 NLT). I think when we finally get a chance to see the true condition of our soul without Christ, we will run to Him, clinging desperately to faith in His sacrifice, and declare on that day, "*The Lord* is [MY] righteousness" (Jeremiah 23:6 NLT, emphasis mine).

To Know Him

The confidence you have in God is determined by the foundation of forgiveness and grace He builds in your heart. Without true knowledge and experience of His grace you can only hope to walk blindly through this life, guessing at who you believe God is. However, if you seek to embrace all He is as your Savior, you will walk boldly in His power and authority, knowing you are, indeed, *a brand new creation in Christ.*

As you are re-created in His likeness, you radiate His glory and He displays *you* as a part of His glorious robe – reflecting His glory to generations. He proudly presents you, His most precious treasure, a part of Himself. One with Him, you've been transformed, enveloped and blended as one with the fibers of His glorious robe – a living treasure, a reflection of His grace.

Can We Trust Him?

As you realize how much He loves you, you will walk in a greater degree of the power and authority of His presence. Then His radiant, glorious light will shine through you before all men, and your heavenly Father will receive praise (see Matthew 5:16).

Beloved, you do not put your faith in a *little* God, but the One who created all things. He really is an awe-inspiring God, and the promise of His presence is no small thing. He laid the foundations of the earth and commands the sun to rise each morning. He tells the seas how far to come to shore and understands the expanse of the universe (see Job 38:4-18).

As you seek God and wait for Him, your faith increases and you are no longer limited by this natural earthly world. The disciples were told to wait for His presence to come to them; He promised them power as they experienced His presence (Acts 1:4). That same power is yours today; you can experience the promise every day by waiting on Him – seeking Him. As you determine to live in Him, His power and authority will follow your life. Indeed, His creative power is made available to you.

16

Mysterious Love

TO THOSE who overcome in the midst of adversity, He will give increased authority (see Revelation 2:26).

If you have been tried in the fires of adversity I'm sure you've discovered that in those times, as you thrust yourself into the bosom of your Father, you walk away having learned the secrets of His heart. It is in leaning into Him in exhausted desperation that you truly find the depth of His love for you.

I clung to this revelation for years as I went through a lengthy onslaught of painful accusations. I had asked God to weed out my need for approval from others, which seemed to be rooted in my people-pleasing nature.

However, as the pain of the endless accusations seemed to crush my heart at times, I would cry to God, "Why is this happening to me?"

He answered time and again, "It will be worth it."

It took me a long time to really see the weaknesses that were in me, but God knew just how important it was that these issues in my life were confronted and fought, because they were a danger to my future. It did hurt ... a lot, and sometimes it still does.

For years, I was repeatedly lied about, misunderstood and in general just hated. I didn't understand why it was happening. Finally, the Lord *mercifully* gave me the following vision. It helped me so much. It made me love Him even more, because no matter what we endure, we have not endured as much as He has. As He has guided and loved each of us through crucifixion-like trials, He has endured the brunt of the attack for us.

Liquid Fire *A Vision*

I walked with Jesus along a long and treacherous path. As we walked He kept His arm around me, but in His other arm He held a large gold cross-encrusted shield. He held the shield high and protected us both, deflecting many fiery darts shot at us from demonically influenced people on every side.

Under a heavy onslaught of blazing arrows of accusation, condemnation and unrighteous judgment, we walked together toward our destination. We were assaulted by dear Christian friends who, believing the lies the demons were feeding them, passionately ripped at my heart. Leaving little of my life untouched, they had been attacked by a deceptive demon whose purpose was to cause me harm by working through them.

Jesus was able to deflect many of the darts with His shield, but sometimes the arrows would hit me and I felt my body writhe in pain. At first the pain shocked me, making me unable to move or respond to their actions. But as I gained control of my senses, I became so angry I wanted to lash out at them.

The more I tried to defend myself, the greater the attack became. Pelted by accusation, the Lord grabbed me and turned me into Himself until my face was buried in His chest. He held me there for a while, absorbing some of the pain of the attack into Himself, restoring my mind and spirit with His.

We crept along the path for some time, as the lies and accusations of the enemy continued to rage against me. I didn't understand why the battle was targeted against me, what caused it, or how to get it to stop. All I did know was that I needed to stay with Jesus because, in the midst of this fierce battle, I was safe with Him.

As I looked ahead, I could see a faint light in the distance. The longer we walked, the greater the light became. The closer we got to the light the less the battle could affect us, until finally we reached God's throne.

I could feel the kindness and severity of God as we drew near the throne. As we approached the Father, the

Lord continued to hold me close while He urged me to step forward.

Jesus spoke to Him, "Dearest Father, this child has faithfully passed through the pathway of accusation and is worthy of Your blessing. Will you please bless her?"

The Father reached His arm out toward me and from the palm of His hand came drops of white liquid fire, which seemed to make up His whole being. As the drops of fire hit me, they went through my body until suddenly I lost all strength and could no longer stand. Falling to the floor, I wept before Him as the drops continued to wash through my soul until He pulled back His hand and the drops ceased.

Lying on the floor weeping and unable to move, I felt Jesus wrapping His arms around me, picking me up and helping me to my feet. Slowly and quietly He carried me to a small hill nearby, where we sat down and talked together. Still embracing me, He told me of my future. He said, "The Father and I have planned for you to stand on this hill. As you stand here, we will bring people to you so they can experience the Father's glorious fire, as they are restored and prepared for their destiny. Will you help them find Me?" Still shaking and weak from the Father's touch, I nodded my head yes as He left me to rest on the grass-covered hill.

As I lay there, I began to think back on our journey down the pathway. The accusations still pained me until

I realized that Jesus had taken a much more difficult journey to Golgotha through the enemy's accusations. And He made it alone, without a shield. Although the battle I had endured was difficult, it would have been much more so had Jesus not been there with me to defend me.

Peace filled my soul as I remembered the words in 1 Peter 2:21-23, "For you have been called for this purpose, since Christ also suffered for you, leaving you an example for you to follow in His steps, who committed no sin, nor was any deceit found in His mouth; *and while being reviled, He did not revile in return; while suffering, He uttered no threats, but kept entrusting Himself to Him who judges righteously*" (NASB).

If you are walking on a similar path, it cannot keep you from the plan God has for your life. The journey of accusation is devastating and debilitating, it can leave your heart broken beyond what you feel God is able to restore, but He *will* restore you. Remember the prize – there is nothing that compares to His splendor.

The accusations of the enemy cannot keep you from Him. In fact, they can even help you receive more of Him, as His Word says, "The Lord is near to the brokenhearted" (Psalm 34:18 NASB). Though the battle rages all around you, stay close to your Savior, for in Him you will find refuge and strength.

No matter what the cost, His glory is worth the struggle, for "a day in [His] courts is better than a thousand outside" (Psalm 84:10 NASB, emphasis mine). Though men accuse you and believe all manner of evil against you, there is nothing that can keep you from the love of your heavenly Father.

> For I am convinced that neither death, nor life, nor angels, nor principalities, nor things present, nor things to come, nor powers, nor height, nor depth, nor any other created thing, will be able to separate us from the love of God, which is in Christ Jesus our Lord.   —Romans 8:38 NASB

The Finisher

"Jesus, the author and finisher of our faith" (Hebrews 12:2 NKJV). An author drafts a manuscript, but the original writing is often flawed and unpolished. It takes a great deal of work to get to the finished work. God only finishes what He values – if the manuscript He's written (that's you) is worthy and valuable, then He gets excited and says, "We can work with this!" It doesn't mean you are ready for print just yet, but it does mean He sees great promise in you and wants to focus attention on you. It may be difficult, but don't feel picked on; feel valued.

It's like a gardener who works for years to develop that one perfect rose, pruning and fertilizing it, making sure it's in just the right location for growth. Finally, the gardener experiences great joy when at last he sees the fruit of his labors in the culmination of his ideal rose.

God works in us much the same way. He works hard developing us as He prunes, weeds, refines, replants, digs and fertilizes, until after years of work He is rewarded with that one perfect rose: You! And all that God has built into you is held in the "fragrance" you radiate to the world.

Every time you've endured a breaking experience, you are refined (see James 1:2) and made even more beautiful still. It's true. He's the Author and the Finisher, and He will bring you through your beginnings to a desirable end. He knows you will become like Him. What a joyous thought! God believes in you. His goal for you is to become like Him.

17

My Beloved

And I saw between the throne (with the four living creatures) and the elders a Lamb standing, as if slain.   —Revelation 5:6 NASB

Driven to the Cross

In John's vision of heaven in Revelation 5, he saw a Lamb who had been slain, yet He stood. He was dead, yet He lived. He was the fearsome King of heaven, our King Jesus.

Jesus Christ was driven to the Cross out of love for you. Truly, all hell came against Him, yet He stood in awesome triumph over His enemies. Not even death could hold Him; the grave could not keep Him. Victory was His destiny and now He stands, having triumphed over His enemies and taken His rightful place at the throne of heaven.

When the enemy attacks you, harassing and wounding you, understand that your champion Christ has positioned Himself as your refuge. And no matter what hell throws at you – no matter how the enemy targets you, you will be transformed as you are driven into Christ's presence. His love makes you victorious and transforms you into the new creation He's designed for you to become – a powerful, eternal being destined to champion earth.

Kingdom Bride

In a vision, my youngest son, Cole, saw a woman whom the enemy had entangled in chains. She was held captive by the chains that bound her. I believe this vision is how the bride of Christ has looked for many years, and the church is still very much entangled in the world and even enslaved by it. The enemy wants us to see ourselves as his property – caught by his sin, yet we are indeed eternal beings made in the image of God.

Truly, when you see yourself according to how people treat you, you will lose sight of your true value. You are beloved of the Father. You are not unworthy of love and respect; you may not get respect from others, but you can at least let God love you. Only then will you begin to see yourself the way He does and start believing you can accomplish your destiny. You were created to reign, not to be dominated and trampled by this world, but if you're not vigilant that is exactly what the enemy would have you believe about yourself.

Satan has plans for your life and he will use anything or any one to further his plans. He wants you to feel rejected and despised, unappealing and inadequate; he wants you to feel this way because he's terrified of you. But the harassment of the enemy will only push you to find refuge in the One who loves you and is your shelter.

God sees the real you, the lovely you, and He wants you to see it, too. He wants to reveal your loveliness to yourself and to the world.

You *are* the bride of heaven and, though all hell rages against you, you will overcome and become His kingdom bride as you cling to Him. He has designed a special and unique destiny for your life. He intends to equip and prepare you for it. Though you may endure a season of rejection, you will indeed begin to find your worth in Christ alone, not in the storms that surround you. You will cast off the chains of the enemy and turn and strangle him with them.

Driven to Prison for God's Purposes

"Dear brothers and sisters, when troubles come your way, consider it an opportunity for great joy. For you know that when your faith is tested, your endurance has a chance to grow. So let it grow, for when your endurance is fully developed, you will be perfect and complete, needing nothing" (James 1:2-4 NLT).

Joseph, in Genesis, was betrayed by his brothers and spent 13 years as a slave – as someone's property (Genesis 37:21-28) and then as a prisoner. He was accused of being a degenerate, going after his master's wife, when in reality the opposite was true (Genesis 39:6-20). His life as he knew it had been stripped from him physically and emotionally; no longer a most beloved, favored son. He was someone's property, and then wrongfully imprisoned.

If anyone had the right to become angry and bitter, it was Joseph. The Lord had shown him amazing visions and dreams of all he would do in his future (Genesis 37:5-11). However, his life went in the complete opposite direction for years. But Joseph clung to God and trusted Him during the storms in his life (Genesis 39:2-5 and Genesis 39:21-23).

As Joseph sat in prison for years, it may have seemed that he was never going to fulfill the dream he'd had for his life, and yet all that had happened to him drove him into the very place where he was needed. His enemies pushed him to the throne of Pharaoh.

All that was taken from him and done to him turned out to be the preparation for the fulfillment of his dreams (Genesis 45:5-8). Joseph endured a life of dramatic change; he went from being the favored son of his father to a lowly slave and prisoner, and then suddenly became second in power over Egypt (Genesis 45:8) and used by God to save millions.

Driven to a Cave

David worshipped God in an uncharacterized fashion for his time. No one was worshipping God as intensely and intimately as David. Most all the children of Israel worshipped God with sacrifices of animals, but David gave God the praise due Him. He knew God didn't want sacrifices as much as He wanted His children to love and obey Him (Psalm 40:6). So David did.

David was blessed when Samuel anointed him to be king of all Israel. Though this in itself was a tremendous blessing and honor for him, it started him on an irreversible path of destiny. How does God make a king? He started first with a person He loved, a beautiful shepherd boy who worshipped with all his heart (1 Samuel 16:11). Then He made him a great warrior (1 Samuel 18:5-7) and son-in-law to the king (1 Samuel 18:17-27).

However, David suddenly endured what seemed to be a reversal of fortune, becoming an escaped fugitive running for his life (1 Samuel 19-24), living in caves (1 Samuel 22:1-2), pretending to be a madman (1 Samuel 21:13), having his wives taken from him and being despised and rejected (1 Samuel 30:1-6).

David was pursued by those who had every reason to love him but wanted him dead. His enemies drove him into a cave where he hid until God was ready for him to be made king of all Israel (2 Samuel 5:1-5).

David's cave was disgusting in the natural, but it was the evidence of God's love and favor on him. God loved David and sent him to the cave, not just to escape his enemy but to become a very great king. It sounds ridiculous to say God uses caves to make kings, and He doesn't always. He uses caves to make kings He absolutely loves and adores with all His heart. He protected David's life in the cave but He also protected his future, because He loved him.

David was created to reign by the trials he faced. He was made great by steadfastly serving God even in the gravest circumstances.

Clinging to God's Love

Maybe you have had similar experiences in your life and are now living in a "cave" of sorts. You've been shaken and rocked to your core until you feel emotionally numb. Yet, though you may have been stripped, robbed or betrayed, you've clung to God and discovered in the midst of your desperation that you still have the one thing that truly matters – you still have God.

Suddenly, you realized He is your *everything* and, spiritually speaking, you've become one of the wealthiest people in the world. When you realize your true wealth in Him, you have the strength to handle the authority of the position God needs you to fulfill. The pressure will be great, and He does not want to lose you in the midst of it all. So, He made sure your foundation was rock solid in Him (Revelation 3:19).

David, Joseph and countless others changed their lives as they clung to God. Your story, too, takes on a new and rich purpose when you cling to Him. Driven into His presence, you are made new, including the pain of your past. You are made beautiful from the ashes of your life (Isaiah 61:3).

You are made victorious through the storm, for as the enemy harasses you, you run deeper into your Lord. And as you run to Him, desperate to find a refuge from the attacks of the enemy, you realize that in pursuing you, the enemy's driven you to become what God destined for you to be.

Driven into His Presence! *A Vision*

Before an impending attack against my family, the Lord revealed to me the end result of the attack. He gave me this beautiful vision of the bride of Jesus Christ called Beloved.

I saw Beloved running, dressed in the most exquisite gown I'd ever seen; it was breathtaking. Made of sheer organza, it had a graceful train and sleeves that grazed the ground. Beloved was very stunning with long, beautiful auburn hair that seemed to flow into her gown.

She was running from something chasing her; she was frightened and wanted desperately to get away. Shrouded in darkness, I could not see clearly what was chasing her, but knew it was dangerous. It came very close to catching her at times and yet as it did, her desperation to escape its grasp drove her harder to stay out of its reach.

As she searched for a safe place to run, she spotted an open door leading to a rustic stone staircase. The opening of the doorway was at first hidden from her, but she ran toward it in hopes it would be a place she could hide. It appeared quite ominous but when she realized it was open she felt a glimmer of hope and ran toward it.

As Beloved reached the door, she dashed for the stairs without hesitation. Still, three intimidating shadows lurked closely behind her and I could see they were determined to get hold of her.

She continued up the stairs of the old building, climbing and gasping as she went, looking back only occasionally. She continued to run, yet started losing ground – they were gaining on her. She realized her only hope to escape them was to climb higher and keep her focus on what lay ahead.

Suddenly, a ray of light from the top of the stairs fell on her face. It caught her attention and as she focused on it, hope rose in her heart. She climbed higher and higher, creating a greater distance between her and the creatures that pursued her.

As she ran from them, her expectation at what lay ahead increased. She could see more clearly where she was running and was even more certain there would be a place of refuge for her there. Continuing to run, the train of her gown grew longer and even more radiant. She seldom looked behind her now, and the higher she went the more difficult it was for them to follow.

Her desperation began to fade from her heart as joyful anticipation filled her, making her even more beautiful. She knew she would make it and was filled with expectancy, increasing her confidence and strength.

Exhausted and trailing at a great distance, the creatures continued to pursue her. They were instinctively compelled to chase even though they had little hope of catching her.

The Light

Beloved's attention was completely fixed on what lay ahead of her now. When she first saw the stairs, she could see nothing but a hoped-for escape from her enemies. Yet, now she was captivated by the brilliant light that burned before her. It was distant, but it was there; seeing it filled her heart with joy. As her hope grew, her beauty increased. The train of her gown continued to grow as she persisted in climbing toward the light.

Running with joyous longing, she continued, with every step bringing her closer to the light she saw. She began to realize that as she approached the Light, it was more to her than just a refuge from her pursuers. It was the Light of her Dearest Joy, and in Him lay her destiny – her completeness – her total fulfillment – her Lord.

The Light was pouring down on her now and gave her strength to reach higher. Thoughts flooded her mind as the Light filled her: He loved her – He would protect her – she was important to Him – she had a purpose – He had a plan – He wanted to be her everything – healing power filled her mind, heart and soul. Her eyes were raised to Him – her lips released praise.

She pushed herself harder and harder, not out of fear but inexpressible joy. Love filled her heart and brought healing to her wounds. Confidence filled her legs and she flew faster and faster, racing toward Him – her Dearest – her Everything – her Beloved.

Nothing else mattered but Him – *He was everything to her, and she was His whole heart.*

She felt Him now; His heart drew her to Him. She was His world – beautiful – radiant. He wanted to hold her – protect her – and she was coming to Him. She was reaching for Him, needing Him, wanting Him and loving Him.

She had run with only a hope of Him, not even sure of His existence, and her love was more precious to Him because of it. Her faith touched His heart and He wanted to cry for her, but His cry went deep inside of Him, deep down inside, as His face looked up to His Father. He was filled with a bright, captivating light.

The Light swelled His chest and burst out from Him all around like a powerful explosion. As it shot out, like long arms of light, it exploded in all directions. The light that radiated from Him reached out to her and embraced her, drawing her instantly to Himself.

He wrapped her in His embrace, burying her in light. She closed her eyes and hid her face in Him. She was safe with Him at last.

Everything – all – complete – shelter – one – life – love – all of these things filled her. She was with Him in a place of safety... a place of rest.

Mercy

Jesus saw them first, as they came trailing up the stairs after her. She turned to follow His gaze and saw the creatures again as they approached. She was not frightened of them now. Indeed, she pitied them. They had harassed her, trying to keep her from her destiny and make her what they wanted her to be. Yet, as frightening as they used to be to her, they looked small and pitiful to her now.

They stood back, unaccustomed to the light, suddenly discovering they knew little of why they had come; they paused awkwardly before the radiant pair.

Watching them and pitying them, she turned to Jesus and looked into His eyes. Without having said a word to Him, He understood her desire. Receiving her gaze, He gave her a knowing glance. In response, He gently pulled back from her and gave out a tremendous roar.

Suddenly, His body was filled with fire and He transformed into a ferocious Lion of fire. His roar shot out of Him and saturated the creatures standing before Him. They braced themselves to receive the blow, indeed almost welcoming it.

Instantly, the fire of His roar consumed the creatures; smoke and ash filled the space where they once stood. The air snapped with sparks from the blaze and smelled like sulfur.

Beloved's eyes watched; there was a strange yet tranquil light coming from three people who knelt now where the creatures stood only moments before.

The creatures had been human all along and now were once again. In humble penitence they knelt before Him. He had mercy on them and transformed them, returning them to what they had been previously, before sin had distorted them.

WOW

Understanding and thankfulness filled them now as they worshipped at His feet, grateful to be set free.

Driven to Be His Own

The enemy has harassed and assaulted the beloved of the Lord (the bride of Christ – *you*), seeking to use you for His own purposes. Because of God's love for you, the enemy will stop at nothing to deter you from your relationship with Him, from your purpose and oneness with your Lord. He will use anyone or anything, even your own desires, to keep you from Him.

Yet, the very wounds the enemy inflicts and the dangers which surround you will fatefully drive you deeper into the arms of your Dearest Lord even if it means finding refuge in a cave. Your longing could lead you anywhere, because even a cave becomes paradise when He is with you.

Your enemy wants to destroy you, to chase you from your Lord, yet now you find your head buried in His chest and you are lit from within by the glory of His love; you are infused with Him, and the enemy cannot have you. And truly, the overwhelming light of heaven will captivate even the hardest, vilest heart, releasing them from the torturous darkness that binds them.

Beloved, please trust that God loves you very much and that He is passionately pursuing you. He desperately wants you for His own.

18

A Light to the World

WHEN THE SON of Mary and Joseph first came into the world, many people accepted Him as being a man of God. Later, they welcomed the healing and deliverance He brought them. They embraced His wisdom. They enjoyed the blessing of the miracles He performed. But when Jesus said He was the Bread of Life (see John 6:35), they turned their backs on Him (see John 6:66). When He referred to Himself as the Light of the World (see John 8:12), they thought He was demon-possessed (see John 8:48). When He promised them eternal life through His life (see John 6:54), it was a difficult concept for them to grasp.

However, it was more important that *Jesus* knew who He was than convincing the masses of who He was. He was confident in His calling. He was kingdom-minded and purpose driven. He knew what it was He was after and He would let nothing get in His way. His purpose was to plunder Satan's domain and plant Himself as a seed in the earth. He was not living for His life on this earth, He saw a much bigger picture. He saw eternity and He wanted you with Him.

If Christ dwells in you, you are truly the light of the world. God has chosen to show Himself to the world through you. You are called to know Him, love Him and through your love, reveal His heart to the world.

Living as He Lived

Yet, to display His power and glory on earth, you must live as a stranger to this world. Thank God this world is not your home. Indeed, your home is with your heavenly Father. You are His well-beloved child, living as He would – in this world, not by its standards but by the standards of your heavenly home. Living like the world puts an unfortunate barrier between yourself and God (see James 4:4), dimming your power to influence or change it.

You are in this world, but you truly are not of it. Once you belong to God, you are a part of the kingdom of heaven and bear the light of heaven. You are His heir. As an heir of His kingdom, though living here in this world, you are an administrator of the will of the heavenly realm. Be always mindful that you are His ambassador here, not a resident. And as Christ shines

through you, this world will see a difference in you and
run to you as a representive of Jesus Christ. ￼

The Hope of Heaven!

You are the *hope* of heaven (Colossians 1:27)! God
has entrusted you with the deeply significant task
of bringing His light to the world. Indeed, it's not a
religion that will light the world, but the love of God
shining through you. And every prayer you pray, every
word you speak – every decision you make in your life
– should be made with the understanding of the reality
of your heavenly calling.

God is looking for those who will *lose their lives*, but
find *life in Him* in the process. Man or woman, rich or
poor, slave or free, Jew or Gentile, it does not matter
(see Galatians 3:28). Will you accept this calling? Will
you let it change you? Will you give Him your life, your
choices, your fears and even your failings?

If you give up your earthly life – the plans that you
have made for yourself – and embrace the life He has for
you, you will find in return a life greater than you've ever
dreamed of (see Matthew 10:39). Only then can you walk
as Jesus walked, in the love He walked in. Indeed, you
will lay hands on the sick and they *will* recover, because
you will know that it was for this purpose you were born.
As God sent His Son into the world as a light, so you are
sent as a light to help others find their way to Him.

The great crowd of witnesses in heaven is waiting to see what you will do next. They are even now crying to God to raise up men and women who will shine the light of Jesus Christ to a dark world – to their loved ones here on earth. And the light of Jesus shining through you is their hope (see Colossians 1:27).

> Therefore, since we are surrounded by such a huge crowd of witnesses to the life of faith, let us strip off every weight that slows us down, especially the sin that so easily trips us up. And let us run with endurance the race God has set before us.
>
> —Hebrews 12:1 NLT

His Dwelling Place

You are the resting place of God – His holy place (Isaiah 66:1). God does not live in a house made by human hands, but He has built His home in you. You are the dwelling place of God – the showcase for His glory; in your heart He feels at home.

In the temple that Solomon built, there were many places for the people to come and worship. But the Holy of Holies was reserved for God's glory. Those who would enter His holy place must first purify themselves or they would die because of the intensity of His glory. And to make Him comfortable in your heart – His dwelling place (see 1 Corinthians 3:16) – you too must keep your heart pure.

The blood of the Lamb purifies you, and you now live as a sacred vessel set apart for His purposes. You are not to live as the world does, but as Christ would – not out of pride but in humility as an act of love and worship to Him. God is looking for a place to rest, a place where His Spirit can dwell. He wants that place to be in you. He wants His glory to dwell in you and radiate from you, to make your heart His home.

You are the light of the world – the salt of the earth – a city set on a hill (see Matthew 5:13-14). Without you, the earth has lost its light and heaven has no hope. You are important and as you live *for* Him and *in* Him and *through* Him, you light the world.

That is beautiful

The World Is Fading

Do not love this world nor the things it offers you, for when you love the world, you do not have the love of the Father in you. For the world offers only a craving for physical pleasure, a craving for everything we see, and pride in our achievements and possessions. These are not from the Father, but are from this world. And this world is fading away, along with everything that people crave. But anyone who does what pleases God will live forever. *WOW*   —1 John 2:15-18 NLT

This world, as we know it, is scheduled for destruction – it's fading fast. Building your life in this world is futile when you consider you'll only be able to enjoy the fruit of your labor for a few years, compared to eternity. Life on this earth is short – a mere breath or vapor; eternity is forever.

Your precious life spent to work for mere earthly success is a waste of how remarkable you are. What the world sees as success is a waste in God's eyes because He sees your true potential. You were made for a sacred purpose – to rule this world as well as the next.

You were made for eternal significance. And as the kingdoms of the earth become the kingdoms of our God (see Revelation 11:15) you were destined to reign with Him forever and forever.

The world *is* fading fast, and the enemy wants to get your focus off the eternal kingdom of God and onto the temporal concerns of this world – busying you with things that will not last and can never fulfill you. You were made for eternity. You were made for God's family – to dwell with Him. You are royalty, made to adorn a palace. Nothing this earth has can compare to your true destiny in Him.

An Unseen War

Did you know you are an eternal being? Did you know your neighbor is?

Your treasure is here waiting for you to claim it. God says, "Ask Me" for the nations (Psalm 2:8). He wants you to ask Him for ALL He has for you - He wants you to believe Him for a significant breakthrough in the lives of those without hope.

We are in an unseen war, whether we want it or not, and that war is being fought all around us; indeed, the war is fought for the souls of men on earth. The enemy is intent on slandering God as he's done since the time of Genesis; this dreadful accusation and slander is his main weapon against our God.

Of course the enemy is content to let people believe in God - to believe He exists, but his main onslaught against God's kingdom is an attack against the true nature of God and His relationship with humanity. So you see, your mission is made clear: *to show the world God's love.* WOW

Surely, if the lost could realize His real affection for them, they would know there is more to Him than what they've experienced. Then He could fill the empty void in their soul, dwelling in them as the very temple and dwelling place of God (1 Corinthians 3:16).

As they experience His true feelings for them, sin can no longer hold them. The grip of shame is power-less against God's all consuming, unconditional love; Satan's plan for their life is exposed and shattered.

God's dream for you is to show you that you have the power in you to change a life and the world.

You are the light of heaven sent to a very dark world to administrate the government of heaven and to bring His heavenly purposes to this earth – to set the captives free! You are the gateway to bringing the reality of heaven to the earth – to calling the nations to the light of Christ and making Him known to them as He truly is.

God has not given up on His desire for intimacy with His beloved – of dwelling with you as He did with man in the Garden of Eden. Satan tried to stop your Father's plan, but God will never back down. He cannot, because He is anticipating the joy of you – His well-beloved child. And He has made you to shine brightly – radiating His presence and His love. Nothing on this earth will stop His love from reaching you, because He knows "Christ in you, the hope of glory" (Colossians 1:27).

19

Our Mission

IF YOU WANT to experience more of God's presence in your life, then you need only to love others. "But if we love each other, God lives in us, and his love is brought to full expression in us (1 John 4:12 NLT).

Loving His people enables you to feel His presence to a greater extent. "Anyone who loves another brother or sister is living in the light" (1 John 2:10). And you can see and feel God in even the simplest things on this earth if you have His love, because if you love His people, you will see Him.

One act of kindness can produce more of God's presence in your life than any other Christian act. Love is a powerful force, for as you do unto the least of these, you experience God.

Ambassadors of Love

"God showed how much he loved us by sending his one and only Son into the world so that we might have eternal life through him" (1 John 4:9 NLT).

God sent Jesus to you to show you what true love looks like. His idea was that He would send His Son to give an example of how to love so you and I could become like Him. The Father then intends that, just as Christ was God's ambassador of His love, we would become Christ's ambassador of that same amazing love.

As you pursue God, His love becomes your motivation for everything in your life, because God is love. As He imparts Himself to you, you can't help but love others. You will see not only yourself in His light, you will also see others as He sees them – as they truly are (1 John 2:9). With the light of His love in your heart, you see rightly; as you walk in His light your heart is open to seeing the *true* value in others. As you prefer one another you see the righteousness of God shine through you.

Maturing Love

God is love and as you practice love, you will know Him more. Satan knows how powerful love is and how it can empower you, so his goal is to wound your love, even causing you to fear it, if he can. Unfortunately, he's very good at causing pain. Indeed, offense can tear up the groundwork that love has lain in your life, but even this can become an occasion for God's presence to increase in your life.

When you choose to love even those who've hurt you, your forgiveness releases a powerful dose of God's presence in your life; He will honor you and free you. Offense seeks to bind you and keep your love from flowing. But when you free yourself from the chains of offense and love in spite of wrongs done to you, His spirit explodes within you.

God is close to the brokenhearted and during times of pain or betrayal, your love is maturing, increasing and becoming even more powerful. It is inevitable that you will go through the valley of offense from time to time (John 16:33), but every time you do, your love grows deeper. Your relationship with Him becomes more intimate because He is love and, "Whoever lives in love lives in God, and God in them" (1 John 4:16).

To walk in His presence, you have to allow Him to change your mind about others, to help you forgive and love again. It is not often an easy thing, and you will have to battle the enemy as you let God tear down the walls of judgment, bitterness and pain that have risen in your heart. You battle not with the people who've offended you in the natural, but with your own heart. And as you are victorious over your own heart and mind, you will realize God has replaced the pain you felt with the power of His Spirit, equipping you to be His champion of love.

It's easy for your heart to become hardened. Without even realizing it your heart turns inward to protect itself when you've been hurt, but to shut it up with anger, pain or fear isn't the answer. God understands your pain and loves you even when you are angry.

He wants you to let go of your pain, loneliness and despair; give it to Him. If you hold onto offense, it will drive you away from Him. Living separated from God opens your heart to spiritual darkness that is easily exploited by the enemy. It's a terrible place to be. In the darkness, you could end up doing things you'd never do in the light. It is far too easy to strike out at what you cannot really see because the darkness has blinded you.

Yet, through asking for the spirit of forgiveness to dwell in your heart, your conscience is able to feel again. The darkness is soon exposed, freeing you from your fear through the safety of His love.

Certainly, to love and forgive is a battle, but it is a battle you cannot fight on your own. Only by asking God to help you love can you overcome. He has overcome and will give you His strength as you need it. Just ask Him for it.

God's Love for the Lost

God hates sin because of the effect it has on His creation. It causes Him great pain to watch those He dearly loves fall into sin that will damage and darken their lives, compelling them to turn away from Him. He hates to see you walk into something that will bring you pain, but He will never leave you.

God will never give up on you, even in the darkness of your sin. He will never stop loving you. That's why sin causes Him such pain, because He cannot stop loving you even in the midst of it.

In Germany, after the Holocaust of the Jewish people in WW2, how did God react toward those who tried to annihilate them? He did rescue the Jewish people and He did restore their nation to them, but His love went beyond thinking of the victims of this great evil. God's love continues to seek out those through whom this great evil came to be. He sent and is still sending His love into Germany to minister to and save those who had perpetrated such atrocities against His people. His heart ached for those caught in darkness who had tried to blacken out the apple of His eye (see Zechariah 2:8).

God sought out His children who had been wounded by the war – those who'd been victimized by the ruthlessness of their enemies, but also those who'd been held in the grip of an evil so terrifyingly dark they saw no light at all. For His love saw what few were able to see. He saw an incredible evil gripping their hearts and He fought to redeem them from it.

Hold Onto God's Love

There are always reasons why people make the choices they make – maybe an incident that started them on the path they are on. God knows all they have endured and what's made them who they are. He's desperate to rescue them, because He sees all of us through eyes of love.

Satan has conspired to twist the world's view of God, making them believe God is cold and heartless. He's desperate to keep them from experiencing God's love. So he twists the minds of people, making them feel as though it is God who is their real enemy.

It's far too easy to stumble into a "Pharisaic" mind-set of "destroy the sinner." Truly, that's what Satan wants you to do. In fact, his plan quite often is to cause the lost to come against you, wound you and persecute you as he tries to force you to hate them. He knows if you come against them with anger and condemnation, they will run from you, thereby keeping them locked in the darkness he's surrounded them with.

If you fall for his trickery, the enemy's work is complete, causing you to hate those you are called to reach.

Furthermore, he uses their mistrust toward you to make them misunderstand God.

So, this is your battle: to hold onto your love – to hold onto God's unconditional love. Become His champion of love by releasing His captivating power to the lost – a living illustration of the miraculous power of His love.

Father, let Your light shine through mightily to this Your child. Help them to run to You in spite of what they see in the natural. Keep their heart completely focused on You and not on what they can see with their eyes. Continually remind them, Lord, that You are for them and they are Yours. Let their life be filled with continual encounters with You, and may they never be the same again! In Jesus' name.

To contact the author or to order more copies of
His Passionate Pursuit, please visit:
victoriaboyson.com

His Passionate Pursuit is also available at:
The store at XPmedia.com
Amazon.com and other online bookstores
Christian bookstores

For wholesale purchases, please contact:
usaresource@xpmedia.com or
Anchordistributors.com

XPPublishing.com
A ministry of XP Ministries

5-1-21